CROCKPOT RECIPES COOKBOOK

Ketogenic Recipes Full of Low Carb Slow Cooker Meals

(Easy to Prepare Healthy Crock Pot Paleo Recipes)

Gloria Pitts

Published by Alex Howard

© Gloria Pitts

All Rights Reserved

Crockpot Recipes Cookbook: Ketogenic Recipes Full of Low Carb Slow Cooker Meals (Easy to Prepare Healthy Crock Pot Paleo Recipes)

ISBN 978-1-990169-96-0

All rights reserved. No part of this guide may be reproduced in any form without permission in writing from the publisher except in the case of brief quotations embodied in critical articles or reviews.

Legal & Disclaimer

The information contained in this book is not designed to replace or take the place of any form of medicine or professional medical advice. The information in this book has been provided for educational and entertainment purposes only.

The information contained in this book has been compiled from sources deemed reliable, and it is accurate to the best of the Author's knowledge; however, the Author cannot guarantee its accuracy and validity and cannot be held liable for any errors or omissions. Changes are periodically made to this book. You must consult your doctor or get professional medical advice before using any of the suggested remedies, techniques, or information in this book.

Table of contents

Part 1 1

Crockpot Soup Recipes 2
Mexican Chicken Soup 2
Spinach & Vegetable Soup 3
Creamy Pumpkin & Potato Soup 4
Coconut Broccoli Soup 6
Creamy Mushroom Soup 7
Crockpot Beef Recipes 9
Beef Tacos 10
Pasta with Beef Sauce 11
Beef and Mushroom Stew 12
Meatball Sandwiches 14
Creamy White Wine Beef 15
Crockpot Chili Beef 17
Round Beef in Red Wine Gravy 18
Crockpot Chicken Recipes 20
BBQ Pulled Chicken 20
Chicken and Sweet Potato Stew 21
Chinese Style Chicken Salad 22
Chicken Cordon Bleu 24
Green Ginger Chicken Curry 25
Teriyaki Chicken with Pineapple 27
Chicken Breasts with Toasted Almonds 28
Crockpot Pork Recipes 30

- Easy Pork Ragù 30
- Pork Roast with Sauerkraut and Kielbasa 32
- Tangy Pork Chops 33
- Thai Style Ribs 35
- Pork Pozole Verde 37
- Spicy Pork Chops 39
- Italian Shanks in Sauce 41
- Hungarian Style Lamb 43
- Vegetable Sides & Sweets 45
- Crockpot Kale 45
- Mixed Herb Vegetables 47
- Marmalade Glazed Carrots 48
- Fruit & Nut Stuffed Apples 50
- Brandied Fruit Dessert 52
- Baked Vanilla Custard 53
- Bread & Butter Date Pudding 54
- Ginger Poached Pears 56
- Part 2 58
- Introduction 59
- Slow Food – Good Food 60
- 6 Benefits of Slow Cooking 60
- Cooking Measurement Conversion Chart 63
- Optimize your Metabolism 63
- Weight Loss Diet Tips that Really Work 65
- Healthy Breakfast Recipes 66
- Healthy Overnight Steel Cut Oats 66
- Appetizing Chicken Caesar Sandwich 67

Breakfast Sausage Scramble	68
Asian Style Chicken Congee	69
Delicious Oatmeal with Apples	70
Delicious Morning Pudding with Dried Figs	71
Amazing French Toast Casserole	72
Steel-Cut Oats with Honey	73
Breakfast Pumpkin Bread with Cranberries	74
Omelette Casserole	76
Pumpkin Spice Clean Eating Pot Oatmeal	77
Homemade Granola	78
Homemade Greek Yogurt	79
Banana Oatmeal	80
Italian Spicy Omelette	81
Delicious Vegetable and Bacon Quiche	82
Morning Oatmeal with Dried Fruits	84
Delicious Breakfast Hash Brown	85
Easy Potato Breakfast	86
Savory Appetizers	87
Delicious Parmesan-Crusted Chicken	87
Crock Pot Cheese Fondue	89
Mexican Style Chili Colorado Burritos	90
Slow Cooker Chicken Wings	91
Simple BBQ Ribs	92
Classic Beef Lasagna	93
Broccoli & Bacon Cheesy Appetizer	94
Crock Pot Chipotle Chili	95
Crispy Chicken Taquitos	96

Mashed Potatoes	97
Butternut Squash Risotto with Goat Cheese	98
Amazing Mexican Queso Fundid	99
Green Bean Casserole	100
Slow Cooker BBQ Chicken	101
Easy Main Dishes	102
Potatoes with Bacon & Beans	102
Tender Beef and Broccoli	103
Pork Roast in Mustard Sauce	104
Sweet Potato Stew with Chicken	105
Outstanding Sweet Pork	106
Delicious Pork Stew	107
Your Favorite Homemade Potatoes with Pork	108
Honey Chicken with Sesame Seeds	110
Creamy Potatoes with Bratwurst Sausage	112
Delicious Pork Carnitas	114
Sweet Chicken Breast with Honey	116
Asian Pork Chops	117
Slow Cooker Chicken Adobo	119
Famous Santa Fe Chicken	120
Slow Cooker Pork Chops Cacciatore	122
Tender Pork with Herb Vegetables	123
Amazing Tender Chicken with Mushrooms	124
Spicy Pork Chili	125
Zucchini and Tomato Spicy Pasta Sauce	126
Delicious Chicken Penne	127
Adorable Crockpot Italian Chicken	128

Shredded Lime Pork	129
Jerky Chicken	130
Slow Cooker Hawaiian Chicken with Pineapple	131
Potato Stew with Vegetables and Spices	132
Buffalo Chicken Pasta	133
Stuffed Peppers	134
Bacon Cheese Potatoes	135
Pork Chops with Tomatoes	136
Herbs & Wine Veal	137
Tender Pork Chops	138
Delicious Meatballs with Currant Jelly	139
Pork Chops Barbecue with Apples and Onions	139
Hoisin Pork Wraps	140
Black Beans and Beef Stew	141
Asian Pork Chops	143
Apple Cider Beef Roast with Ginger	143
Cabbage and Kielbasa	145
Clean Eating Crock Pot Chuck Roast	145
Roast Pork Loin	147
Slow Cooker Beef Brisket	148
Smoked Up Baby Potatoes with Beef	149
Italian Chicken with Peppers & Spaghetti	151
Delicious Chicken Cordon Bleu	151
Beer Chili Beans with Bratwurst Sausage	152
Salsa Verde Pork	153
Tender Beef Stroganoff	154
Stewed Slow Cooker Round Steak	155

- Sweet Potatoes with Coconut and Pecans 156
- Mom's Amazing Pot Roast 157
- Easy Beef Steak 158
- Effortless Side Dishes 160
- Spicy Quinoa Bowl 160
- Jamaican Curry Chicken 161
- Meaty Tomato Sauce 162
- Delicious Chicken with Mushrooms 163
- Beef and Broccoli Penne 164
- Pesto Chicken with Sun Dried Tomatoes 165
- Amazing Almond Chicken with Curry 166
- Salsa Chicken in Sour Cream 168
- Orange Chicken 169
- Creole Chicken Stew 170
- Creamy Chicken with Noodles 171
- White Chicken Chili 172
- Delicious Chicken with Noodles 173
- Chicken Paprikash Noodles 174
- Amazing Chicken Fajitas Ala Pot 176
- Turkey with Onion-Garlic Sauce 177
- Amazing Soup Recipes 178
- Chicken Soup with Spinach and Herbs 178
- Easy Potato Soup 179
- Simple Pea Soup 180
- Vegetable and Lentil Soup 181
- Spicy Bean Soup with Turkey 182
- Kale Soup with Italian Sausage 182

Potato & Beef Soup 183

Chicken Tomato Soup 185

Black Beans & Ham Soup 186

Delicious Vegetable Soup with Beef Chunks**Error! Bookmark not defined.**

Conclusion 188

Part 1

Crockpot Soup Recipes

Mexican Chicken Soup

Ingredients:

- 10oz chicken meat (about 4 small single pieces of breast meat)
- 8oz Mexican style canned tomatoes
- 14 oz chicken broth (about 2 small cups)
- 3 cloves garlic, minced and roasted
- 1 avocado, chopped
- 1 onion, finely chopped
- 2 cups yellow, green and red bell peppers, chopped
- 1 jalapeno chile pepper, sliced
- ½ cup black olives
- 1 cup tortilla chips (pasta works too)
- salt and black pepper to taste

Directions:

This recipe is an easy to make variation of classical spicy tomato chicken soup. Place everything but the tortilla chips in the crock pot and cook for 3-3½ hours on high heat or for 6-7 hours on low heat. Serve the soup in small bowls topped with tortilla chips, or pasta strips. (If you have ripe home grown tomatoes in the garden, pop one of those in too) Garnish with an avocado slice and sprig of parsley. This soup is packed full of nutrition!

Spinach & Vegetable Soup

Ingredients:

- 1 Tbsp olive or coconut oil
- 2 small finely chopped onions
- 2 chopped carrots
- 1/2 cup of spinach leaves, broken into pieces. (baby spinach leaves are okay)
- 4 pints or about 2 lt. of chicken stock.
- 1 skinned chicken breast meat cut into small pieces. (chicken legs can go in too)

- 2 chopped large sticks of celery
- 1 small peeled swede or parsnip (remove at end of cooking if desired)
- 1/2 tsp ground black pepper
- salt to taste

Directions:

In a skillet on medium heat, saute the onions in the oil for about 3 minutes until lightly golden. Add the carrots and fry for another 3 minutes. Transfer to crock pot and add all the other ingredients. Cook on high for about 4 hours till chicken is tender. Use parsley to garnish, or herbs of your choice. Healthy and delicious!

Creamy Pumpkin & Potato Soup

Ingredients: You need to blend this soup after cooking.

- 1/2 large pumpkin, cut into rough chunks (about 3 - 4 pounds, but flexible)
- 2 large potatoes, peeled and roughly chopped
- 3 sticks celery
- 2 cloves of garlic (optional)
- 3 cups of good chicken stock
- 1 cup hot water
- Salt and black pepper to taste (add about 1 tsp of salt and 1/4 tsp pepper)
- 1/4 cup cream or sour cream (1 Tbsp Philadelphia cream cheese also works well)

Directions:

Cut up all the vegetables into medium to large sized pieces. (They will be blended so don't worry too much about uniformity as long as they are roughly the same size) Place all the vegetables into the crock pot and pour the stock, water and seasonings in. Cook on high for about 4 - 5 hours or till vegetables are tender. Cool slightly, add the cream or Philly cream cheese, then mix to a soup consistency in food processor or with a hand-held blender. Serve immediately. Serves 8 people

Coconut Broccoli Soup

Ingredients: you will need to blend this recipe.

- about 4 large cups raw broccoli florets
- 4 chopped leeks
- 1 chopped brown onion
- 2 shallots, diced
- ¼ apple (diced)
- 2 Tbsp coconut oil (any oil will work)
- 35 fl oz. or 1L chicken stock
- salt to taste
- 1/8 tsp freshly ground black pepper
- 1 cup coconut cream

Directions:

Cut all the broccoli into medium sized pieces. Cut up the leeks, onion and shallots. Peel and dice the apple. Heat oil in large pot; add onions and sauté till soft (not brown, approx. 5-10 mins) Add the broccoli and apple – stir well. Add chicken stock, enough to cover or almost cover the vegetables. Bring to boil then transfer everything into the crock pot, including the seasonings. Slow cook on high for about 3 hours, or low for about 6 until veg is tender. Cool slightly, blend everything with a food processor till smooth, adding the coconut cream at the end. Serve with a dollop of cream or herbs.

Creamy Mushroom Soup

Ingredients:

- 2 Tbs oil or butter
- 1 1/2 pounds or about 750g sliced mushrooms

- 5 - 6 cups good chicken stock
- 1 large onion chopped
- 2 cups cream
- 1/2 clove minced garlic (optional)
- 2 cups whole milk
- 4 Tbsp flour
- salt and black pepper to taste
- fresh herbs for garnish (chives and parsley work well)

Directions:

Heat a pan to medium. Lightly saute the onions in the oil or butter for a few minutes, then toss in the mushrooms and cook for another few minutes. Add chicken stock, garlic and seasonings, stirring to de glaze pan. Place into the crock pot and cook for about 6 - 8 hours on low. About 30 minutes before serving, turn the crock pot up to high and stir in milk and the cream. To thicken the mushroom soup, blend the flour with about 1/4 cup milk and 1/4 cup of soup mix. Stir this through the crock pot mixture. Serve with herbs on top.

Crockpot Beef Recipes

Beef Tacos

Ingredients:

- 2 lbs beef flank, sliced
- 1 onion
- 1 carrot, shredded
- 2 bell peppers (one green, the other red or yellow)
- 1 jalapeno
- salt and black pepper to taste
- other seasoning by your choice (chili powder, cayenne pepper, cumin etc)
- corn tortillas
- avocado
- salsa sauce
- lime juice or fresh lime

Directions:

Finely chop the onion, bell peppers and jalapeno. Mix them with the seasoning of your choice. Rub the beef with this mixture. Turn the heat of your crock pot to low and cook for approximately 8 hours. Once the meat is done, slice it. Make tacos by putting the meat on tortillas. Top each taco with salsa sauce, minced or chopped avocado, shredded carrot and some drops of lime juice.

Pasta with Beef Sauce

Ingredients:

- 2 lbs ground beef
- 1 large onion
- 60oz crushed tomatoes
- 8 oz pasta
- 4 garlic cloves
- ¼ cup grated Parmesan cheese
- 2 Tbsp chopped basil
- salt and black pepper to taste

Directions:

This is a simple, yet delicious slow cooker recipe. Chop the onion in small pieces. Put the ground beef, tomatoes, onion and salt in the crock pot. and cook for 4 hours on high heat or up to 8 hours on low. 30 minutes before the meat sauce is done, add some chopped garlic to the mixture. Meanwhile, boil the pasta. Serve pasta with a big spoon of meat sauce, sprinkle with basil, Parmesan cheese, tomato and basil.

Beef and Mushroom Stew

Ingredients:

- 4 lbs beef chuck steak
- 1 onion
- 1 orange peel
- 1 red and 1 orange bell pepper
- 1 cup beef broth
- 1 cup dry red wine
- ½ cup port or sherry
- 2 Tbsp soy sauce
- ½ tsp chili powder
- 2 tsp thyme

- 1 lb mushrooms
- 2 Tbsp butter
- salt and black pepper to taste
  - broccoli florets optional

Directions:

Finely chop onion, red and orange bell pepper and orange peel. Put them in a frying pan together with broth, wine, port, soy sauce, thyme and chili powder. Let the sauce boil. Meanwhile, cut the meat in about 1in big cubes and place them in a slow cooker. Pour the liquid over the beef and turn your crock pot to high. In 5-6 hours the meat should be very tender. Shortly before the beef is ready, prepare mushrooms. Cut them in a bite-size pieces and fry them for about 15 minutes. Mix the meat and mushrooms together. Serve with rice or potatoes.

Meatball Sandwiches

Ingredients:

- 1 ½ lbs ground beef
- 1 egg
- 2/3 cup chopped onion
- 15oz tomato sauce
- 1/3 cup bread crumbs
- ½ cup chopped green pepper
- 1 Tbsp brown sugar
- 1 Tbsp mustard
- ½ tsp crushed oregano
- 1 tsp chili powder
- salt and pepper to taste
- 8 slightly toasted split sandwich buns
- 2 cups Parmesan cheese, grated

Directions:

Mix together ground beef, egg, bread crumbs, half of the chopped onion, salt, oregano and black pepper in a bowl. Make 32 little meatballs out of the mixture. Put them on a baking pan in a single layer, then bake them in 350° heat for about 20-30 minutes. Meanwhile, in a crock pot stir together tomato sauce, the rest of the onion, brown sugar, mustard, chili powder, salt and pepper. When the meatballs are done, add them to the mixture. Make sure that they are covered with the sauce. Cook on low heat for 3-4 hours or on high heat for 1 ½ or 2 hours. Once the meatballs are done, put them on the sandwich buns. Top the sandwiches with grated Parmesan cheese.

Creamy White Wine Beef

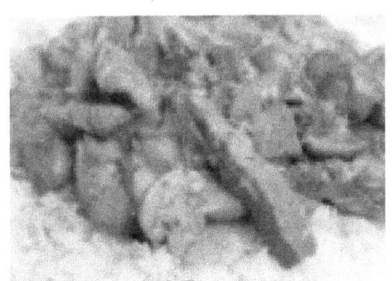

Ingredients:

- 1 ½ lbs round steak

- ½ onion
- 25oz sour cream
- 8oz mushrooms
- 1 Tbsp dried chives
- 1 garlic clove
- ¼ cup dry white wine
- 1 Tbsp flour
- ½ cup fresh dill, roughly cut
- salt and black pepper to taste

Directions:

Cut the beef in strips and place it in a crock pot. Finely chop the onion and pour it over the meat, then add mushrooms and cream. Mix wine with the flour, and add this mixture to the beef too. Finally, season this with chopped garlic, chives, salt and pepper. Cover the pot and cook on low heat for 7 to 8 hours. Can add 1/2 cup of beef stock or water if too dry. Serve with rice or pasta. Season with dill just before serving.

Crockpot Chili Beef

Ingredients:

- 2 Tbsp coconut or olive oil
- 3 1/2 pounds or about 1 1/2 kg lean minced beef
- salt and freshly ground pepper
- 1 large chopped brown onion
- 3 finely chopped cloves garlic
- 2 tsp paprika
- 1/2 finely chopped red chili (1 if you like it hot)
- 1/4 cup chile powder of choice (Mexican, cayenne pepper etc)
- 1/2 Tbsp dried oregano
- 1/2 Tbsp marjoram (can used mixed herbs)
- 1 1/2 tsp ground cumin seeds or powder
- 2 x 28-ounce cans diced tomatoes
- 1 small bottle or stubby of light beer
- 1/2 cup chopped fresh parsley or chives to garnish

Directions:

Heat a fry pan or skillet to medium-high heat. Add 1 Tbsp of the oil and cook the beef for about 3 minutes. Season with salt and pepper, remove and set aside. In same pan add remainder oil and gently fry the onion and garlic for 2 minutes then stir in the chopped chili and cook for a further 2 minutes. Last stir in the paprika but only cook for half a minute so it doesn't go bitter. Take off heat and transfer into crock pot along with the beef, herbs, tomatoes, cumin and beer. Cook on high for about 5 hours, or low about 7. Taste test for salt and pepper, top with fresh herbs for garnish. Serves 6 - 8 people.

Round Beef in Red Wine Gravy

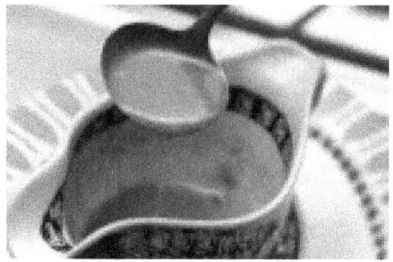

Ingredients:

- 1 Tbsp olive oil

- 3 pound or about 1.3 kg piece round beef
- 2 sliced brown onions
- 5 oz. sliced mushrooms (about 120 gm)
- 2 tea cups beef stock
- 4 minced cloves garlic
- 1/4 cup dry red wine (quality matters!)

For Gravy:

- Mix together 1 1/2 Tbsp arrowroot flour with 1/4 cup the sauce from bottom of crock pot and 1/2 Tbsp favorite BBQ Spice mix (optional - I use a mix of dried herbs with paprika, garlic, pepper, and chili)

Directions:

Heat a heavy based pan to medium high, add the oil and brown the meat well on all sides, for about 6 - 10 minutes. Transfer to the crock pot. In the same pan saute the onions and mushrooms for about 4 minutes. Add the stock, wine and garlic scraping the meaty bits off the bottom of the pan for flavor. Cook on low for about 8 - 10 hours until done. Remove the beef (keep it warm while you make the gravy) Pour all the leftovers from the bottom of crock pot into a saucepan. Heat and stir while you add in the water/flour mix to thicken. Slice meat and top with gravy mix. (You can blend gravy if you want it smooth) Serves 8 people.

Crockpot Chicken Recipes

BBQ Pulled Chicken

Ingredients:

- 2 ½ lbs chicken thighs
- 8oz tomato sauce
- 1 small onion, finely chopped
- 1 clove garlic, minced
- 4oz green chiles, drained
- 3 Tbsp vinegar
- 2 Tbsp honey
- 1 Tbsp Worcestershire sauce
- 2 tsp mustard
- salt and black pepper to taste

Directions:

Warm up and stir the tomato sauce, chiles, vinegar, honey, Worcestershire sauce, mustard, salt and pepper in a crock pot until the sauce becomes smooth. Then mix in onion, garlic and big pieces of chicken. Cover the crock pot and cook everything for approximately 5 hours. Take out the chicken from the sauce. It should be tender by now and easy to shred with a fork. Do it, then mix the chicken shreds back in the sauce. Serve in a burger bun with salad.

Chicken and Sweet Potato Stew

Ingredients:

- 6 chicken thighs, bone-in, skin removed
- 2 lbs sweet potatoes, peeled and cut in large chunks (optional)
- ½ lb Portobello mushrooms, chopped or halved
- 2 big onions, peeled and sliced

- 4 cloves garlic, peeled and sliced
- 1 cup dry white wine
- 2 tsp fresh rosemary, finely chopped
- salt and black pepper to taste

Directions:

This is a very simple, yet delicious recipe. Put everything in the crock pot and cook for 5-6 hours on low heat. Just before serving remove the bones. This stew can be served alone, over rice or with whole grain toasted bread for dipping. Garnish with parsley or fresh herbs of your choice.

Chinese Style Chicken Salad

Ingredients:

- 2 lbs chicken thighs, skin removed
- 8 cups romaine lettuce, shredded
- 1 medium carrot, grated

- ½ medium onion, finely chopped
- 2 celery stalks, finely chopped
- ½ cup cashew nuts, dry-roasted
- 2 cloves garlic, minced
- ½ cup Hoisin sauce
- ¼ cup vinegar
- 2 Tbsp soy sauce
- 2 Tbsp ginger, grated
- 1 Tbsp dry sherry
- 2 tsp chili sauce
- 1 tsp olive oil
- salt and black pepper to taste
- parsley leaves for garnish

Directions:

This is a versatile recipe with ingredients. Use what salads you have handy in the fridge. Place the chicken in a crock pot and sprinkle it with pepper. Add celery, onion and garlic. In a separate bowl mix together Hoisin sauce, soy sauce, chili sauce, sherry, olive oil and grated ginger. Add the sauce to the chicken. Cook the chicken for 2 – 2½ hours on high heat or 5-6 hours on low. When the chicken is tender, take it out of the crock pot and shred it with a fork. For the salad itself, combine romaine lettuce, grated carrot, cashews and chicken in a large bowl. You can use the cooking liquid as the dressing for salad. Garnish with parsley.

Chicken Cordon Bleu

Ingredients:

- 4 chicken breasts
- 4 thin slices of ham
- 4 slices Swiss cheese
- 1 can cream soup (cream-mushroom soup can also be used)
- ¼ cup milk
- salt and black pepper to taste

Optionally:

- 1 egg, whipped
- ½ cup breadcrumbs

Directions:

Flatten the chicken breasts with a mallet until they are thin and tender. On the top of each chicken breast put one slice of ham and one slice of cheese. Create rolls and secure them with a toothpick. Put these chicken rolls in a crock pot. In another bowl stir the soup together with milk until the mixture is even. Then pour it over the chicken rolls. Put the lid on your crock pot, and cook the chicken rolls for 4 hours on low heat. These rolls are ready to eat. However, if you like crunchy chicken, these rolls can also be dipped in egg and breadcrumbs and fried for a short period of time.

Green Ginger Chicken Curry

Ingredients:

- 2 pounds or about 1 kg cubed chicken
- 1 Tbsp olive oil
- 1 large sliced onion
- 1 packet green or yellow curry paste (or your favorite)
- 1 Tbsp shredded coconut
- 1 tsp salt
- 1 small can tomatoes (or about 4 fresh)

- fresh coriander or basil

Paste Ingredients:

- 1 large onion
- 1 tsp coriander seeds
- 1/2 Tbsp peeled and chopped ginger (about 2 inches cubed)
- 5 cloves peeled garlic
- 4 large Kaffir lime leaves

Directions:

Prepare the paste first: Chop up onion into chunks. Place all the 5 "paste ingredients" into a food processor or blender. Blend to make a fairly smooth paste. In a heavy based saucepan or dutch oven pan, over a medium heat, fry 1 sliced onion in the oil. Stir in the green curry paste and stir for a few minutes. Pour the paste mix into the pan and cook for about 4 minutes releasing all the flavors. Now add the cubed chicken stirring as you go and all the remaining ingredients - coconut, tomatoes and salt. Transfer add into the crock pot on low for about 3 hours until done. If mix gets a little dry, add some water or stock. Serves 4 - 6 people. If you like lots of sauce, cut done meat quantity to 1 1/2 pounds. (I make this recipe on the stove top if time permits) Garnish with chili, a tsp of palm sugar or fresh herbs. I like basil mint, or coriander.

Teriyaki Chicken with Pineapple

Ingredients:

- 1 Tbsp oil
- 1 pound chicken breasts (skinless)
- ¼ tsp salt
- ¼ tsp ground black pepper
- 1 diced onion
- 1 diced green capsicum bell pepper
- 1 diced red capsicum capsicum bell pepper
- 1 - 1 1/2 Tbsp soy sauce
- 1/2 tsp ginger, freshly grated
- 1 cup diced pineapple
- 1 cup beans, broccoli or cauliflower

Directions:

Chop the chicken into small 1in pieces, seasoning with salt & pepper. Heat the oil in large frypan. Add chicken and onions; frying over med-high heat. Cook about 5 minutes. Transfer to the crock pot. In the same pan add the soy sauce and ginger cooking for 1 minute. Pour the sauce over the chicken, then place the pineapple, capsicum and vegetables on top. Cook until chicken is completely cooked through and veggies are tender. Serve over chopped cos lettuce and rice or potato.

Chicken Breasts with Toasted Almonds

Ingredients:

- 4 x skinless chicken breast fillets
- 2 tbsp olive oil
- 1/2 chopped onion
- ½ tsp salt

- ½ tsp black pepper
- ⅓ cup slithered almonds
- ½ cup apricots (dried, fresh or canned)
- 1 Tbsp red capsicum pepper diced (optional)
- 1 Tbsp soy sauce
- 1 tbsp mustard

Directions:

Toast slithered almonds on a baking tray for 8-10 minutes till golden or fry lightly in frypan. Set aside. Heat a pan to medium heat. Fry the chicken fillets in the oil for about 5 minutes. Add the onion, salt & pepper, cooking for another 2 - 3 minutes. Place in the crock pot. Combine apricots, soy sauce, mustard and oil in a small bowl and pour over chicken. Now place capsicum or other desired vegetables on top of chicken. Cook on low for about 5 hours till chicken is done. Sprinkle with toasted almonds to serve.

Crockpot Pork Recipes

Easy Pork Ragù

Ingredients:

- 1 ½ lbs boneless pork piece (can used minced pork instead) trimmed and cut in large chunks
- 15oz canned tomatoes
- 1 big carrot, chopped
- 1 medium onion, chopped
- 2 cloves garlic, minced
- 2 Tbsp tomato sauce
- 1 tsp dried thyme
- 1 tsp dried oregano
- ¾ lbs penne pasta
- salt and black pepper to taste
- grated Parmesan cheese (for serving)

Directions:

Combine all the ingredients (except for pasta and Parmesan cheese) in a crock pot and cook until the pork is very tender. (If using mince you will need to stir it or cook on stove top briefly to separate first) It should take about 5-6 hours on high heat or 7-8 hours on low heat. Prepare the penne shortly before serving. It takes approximately 20 minutes for penne to be done. While the pasta is boiling, shred the pork using two forks. Mix it well with the cooking liquid. Once penne is done, drain it and mix with the pork. Sprinkle with Parmesan shortly before serving, and add a few basil leaves for color and added flavor.

Pork Roast with Sauerkraut and Kielbasa

Ingredients:

- 1 ½ lbs boneless pork loin, cut in large chunks
- 4 lbs sauerkraut
- 1 lb kielbasa, cut in bite-size pieces
- 2 Tbsp olive oil
- ½ cup tomato sauce
- ½ cup broth
- salt and black pepper to taste

Directions:

This is a really simple recipe. Place half of the sauerkraut in the crock pot, arrange the kielbasa pieces around the edges and place the pork in the center. Cover everything with the remaining sauerkraut. Pour over the broth and tomato sauce. Put the lid on and cook for 6 hours on high heat.

Tangy Pork Chops

Ingredients:

- 6 pork chops (lamb is also nice instead)
- ½ cup soy sauce
- ¼ cup ketchup or homemade chutney
- ¼ cup brown sugar
- 2 cloves garlic, minced
- 1 tsp ginger, ground
- salt and black pepper to taste
- few spring onions, minced

Directions:

In a bowl combine the soy sauce, ketchup, brown sugar, garlic, ginger, salt and pepper. Stir the mixture until it is even. Place the pork chops in the crock pot and pour over the sauce. Cook on low heat for six hours until the pork chops are nice and tender. Serve the pork chops with the sauce they were cooked in, sprinkle minced spring onions.

Thai Style Ribs

Ingredients:

- 3 ½ pork loin back ribs, cut in large pieces across bones
- 1 can (12 oz) frozen orange, pineapple, apple juice concentrate, thawed
- ¾ cup soy sauce
- ¼ fresh cilantro, finely chopped
- ¼ cup peanut butter
- 2 tsp sugar
- 2 Tbsp ginger, minced
- 1 clove garlic, minced
- salt and black pepper to taste

Directions:

In a large bowl stir all ingredients, but the ribs together. Place the ribs in another bowl and pour the sauce over. Cover the bowl and put it in the refrigerator for 8 hours. Take out the ribs from the marinade and place them in in crock pot. Pour the sauce over and cook on high heat for 1 hour. Then change the heat setting to low and cook for 5 more hours. Serve with the sauce the ribs were cooked in.

Pork Pozole Verde

Ingredients:

- 2 ½ lbs boneless pork shoulder, cut in 1 inch cubes
- 50-60 oz whole tomatillos, drained
- 30 oz drained hominy, or mixed beans, rinsed
- 3 big onions, chopped
- 9 oz green chiles, chopped
- 4 cloves garlic, minced
- ¾ cup chicken broth
- 2 cloves garlic, minced
- 2 tsp ground cumin
- 1 Tbsp sugar
- cooking spray
- oil
- salt and black pepper to taste

Optionally:

- sour cream
- cilantro, chopped
- jalapeno, sliced
- radishes, sliced
  kale, chopped

Directions:

Spray crock pot with cooking spray. Season pork with 1 teaspoon of the cumin, salt and pepper. Heat oil in skillet to high heat and cook the pork pieces for about 7-10 minutes, occasionally stirring. When the pork has browned on all sides, put it in the crock pot. Blend tomatillos with a blender or food processor until smooth. Add them to crock pot among with onions, garlic, green chiles and the remaining cumin. Put lid on the crock pot and cook for 6 hours on low heat. Add hominy or beans of choice and cook for 1 more hour. Serve with sour cream, avocado, cilantro, jalapenos and/or radishes.

Spicy Pork Chops

Ingredients:

- 3 cloves garlic
- 1 small onion
- 1 ½ Tbsp fresh ginger
- 2 tsp Dijon mustard
- 3 tsp Hungarian paprika
- 2 red chilli peppers
- ½ cup apple cider vinegar
- ½ cup good chicken stock
- juice of 1 orange
- ¼ tsp allspice
- 1 Tbsp honey
- 1 ½ Tbsp tomato paste (or 1 fresh tomato)
- 1 cup apple sauce

- 1/2 cup grapes of your choice
- salt & ground black pepper to taste
- 3 – 4 pounds or about 1 1/2 kg pork ribs

Directions:

Place all ingredients except the ribs into a food processor and process for a few minutes (or chop up finely and put in a large bowl). Cut the ribs into manageable sized pieces, 2 ribs per piece works well. Place the ribs into the crock pot and pour the sauce over the top, then place grapes on top. Cook on low for 5 hours until the pork starts to fall away from the bone. Serves 6 people.

Italian Shanks in Sauce

Ingredients:

- 4 - 6 lamb shanks, trimmed of excess fat (I use pork sometimes as it works well too)
- 1/4 cup flour for coating shanks
- 2 Tbsp olive oil
- 2 chopped brown onions
- 4 cloves chopped garlic
- 2 chopped carrots
- 1 Tbsp Italian spicy or BBQ seasoning
- 1/2 red capsicum bell pepper, sliced (optional)
- 1 large potato, peeled and cubed (optional)
- 2 tsp dried mixed herbs (fresh herbs can be used)
- 1 small can diced tomatoes
- 1 cup sliced button mushrooms
- 1 cup beef stock or water
- 1/2 tsp ground black pepper
- 1 tsp salt

Directions:

Toss the shanks in flour that has been seasoned with salt and pepper. Shake off the excess. Heat heavy based pan to medium high. Add half the oil and cook lamb, turning, until browned all over. Transfer to the crock pot. To the same pan on medium heat, use the remainder oil and add the onions, carrots, garlic and herbs, stirring as you go for 2 minutes. Stir in the tomato and stock, bring it to the boil. Pour it all over the lamb shanks in the crock pot. Place the other vegetables on top. Cook on low for 6 - 8 hours until the lamb is starting to come away from the bone. If you want place broccoli or kale on top of the meat. or serve with steamed vegetables. Serves 4 - 6 people.

Hungarian Style Lamb

Ingredients:

- 3 - 4 pound or about 1 1/2kg leg of lamb (trim off excess fat. Pork and beef work well too)
- 2 - 3 fresh rosemary sprigs
- 3 peeled and sliced (length ways) cloves of garlic
- salt and ground black pepper to season
- 1 Tbsp flour
- 1 Tbsp oil
- 1 Tbsp of your favorite chili sauce
- 2 Tbsp honey
- 1 Tbsp paprika

- 1/2 cup stock or water

Directions:

Cut the garlic long ways, in about 8ths. Use a sharp knife to make several incisions all around the lamb. Insert the slivers of garlic and some rosemary into each incision. Season to your taste with plenty of salt and pepper. Coat the lamb with flour. Heat a heavy based pan or skillet to medium high, add half the oil and brown the lamb on all sides. Transfer to the crock pot. In the same pan, over a low heat, add the rest of the oil and stir in the chili, honey, paprika and stock. Stir for a minute de glazing the pan. Bring to boil for a minute. Pour into the crock pot and slow cook on low for 7 - 12 hours depending on size of lamb leg. Turn at about half way through cooking. Serves about 5 - 6 people. (We do this type of dish with pork at Christmas time in the smoker oven outside)

Vegetable Sides & Sweets

Crockpot Kale

Ingredients:

- a bunch of kale, thinly sliced
- 2-3 garlic cloves, finely copped
- 1 small carton or 300g sour cream
- 1 tsp salt
- 2-3 dashes of pepper

Directions:

Warm up (don't boil) the sour cream in a slow cooker. Thinly slice the kale and finely chop the garlic. Once the cream is warm, gently mix in all the ingredients. Simmer everything until the kale is soft. Loaded full of nutrition! Can serve with fine slices of beef, chicken or pork for a meal.

Mixed Herb Vegetables

Ingredients:

- 3 carrots cut lengthways, or whole if small
- 1 cup large chopped pumpkin chunks
- 1 - 2 large quartered or halved potatoes
- 3 spring onions
- 1/2 red chopped capsicum bell pepper
- 1 parsnip (white carrot) cut lengthways, or whole if small (optional)
- 3/4 cup stock
- salt and pepper to taste
- 1/2 tsp garlic flakes or fresh garlic (optional)
- 1/2 tsp dried herbs or fresh herbs

Directions:

Chop the vegetables into similar cooking time sized pieces. Onions can be smaller. Place into the crock pot along with herbs and garlic. Pour the stock and seasoning over the top. Cook on high for about 4 hours until tender. Depends on your vegetable size and crock pot size. Serves about 4 people. Very flexible with which vegetables and herbs you use.

Marmalade Glazed Carrots

Ingredients:

- a packet of about 10 - 12 peeled, sliced carrots
- 1 small cup of water
- 2 Tbsp freshly orange juice
- 1/4 cup homemade marmalade
- 1 Tbsp honey (optional)
- pinch of nutmeg
- 1 tsp mixed or fresh herbs of your choice (mint, sage, marjoram, basil, chives all work well)

Directions:

Cut the carrots into large bite size pieces. Place the carrots and water into the crock pot. Microwave marmalade, nutmeg (honey if using) and juice until it's hot. Cook on high for about 3 - 4 hours until tender, or on low for about 6 hours if you want to eat later. Serves 4 people. This goes beautifully with my Crumbed Cashew Fish recipe here.

Fruit & Nut Stuffed Apples

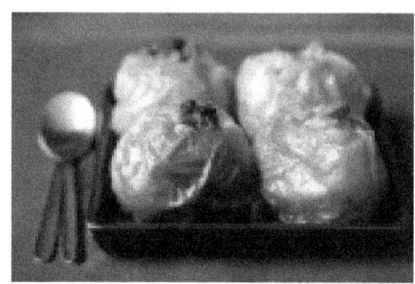

Ingredients:

- 8 cooking apples
- 2 Tbsp honey
- 2 Tbsp dried sultana grapes or currants
- 1/2 cup chopped walnuts, almonds or your choice of unsalted nut
- 1/3 tsp nutmeg (this will be halved)
- 2 tsp cinnamon (this will be halved)
- 2 Tbsp oil or butter
- 1/2 cup apple or orange juice
- squeeze of lemon juice (optional)

Directions:

In a medium sized bowl, mix the honey, dried fruit, nuts, half the cinnamon and half the nutmeg in half the oil. Prepare the apples by coring through the middle and only peeling the top section. Now stuff the nut, fruit and spice mix into the middle of the apples and place into the crock pot. Melt the remaining oil in a pan on a medium heat and add the rest of the cinnamon and nutmeg. Mix the juices together and pour over the apples in the slow cooker. Cook on high for a couple of hours or low, just until tender. Lift out gently when done, allow to stand for a few minutes to firm up. Serves 6 - 8 people.

Brandied Fruit Dessert

Ingredients:

- 2 cups mixed quality dried soft fruits (ideas - apricots, pears, prunes, apples, peaches, cranberries, kiwi fruit, figs)
- 2 Tbsp brown sugar (or sugar alternative)
- 6 chopped dates for sweetness
- 1 cup brandy
- 2 1/2 cups natural apple juice (wine works too)
- zest of 1 lemon
- 1 stick cinnamon or 1 tsp ground (optional)
- 1/4 cup orange liqueur (optional)

Directions:

This is an extravagant cold dessert that I keep in a glass airtight container in the fridge for months...just for special occasions! Put everything into the crock pot and slow cook on low for about 6 - 8 hours, or until the fruit is tender. A trick is if you want to cut down on cooking time, soak fruit overnight (in half the apple juice) beforehand. This recipe is very flexible with ingredients. Remove cinnamon stick before serving with cream, vanilla ice cream or yoghurt. Store in fridge.

Baked Vanilla Custard

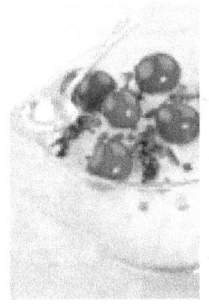

Ingredients:

- 4 large eggs
- 1 1/2 cups full cream milk
- 1/4 cup sugar
- 1 tsp vanilla extract
- 1/4 tsp of ground nutmeg

Directions:
Grease the crock pot dish with butter or oil. In a bowl,

beat the eggs, sugar, milk and vanilla extract together until well combined. Pour into the crock pot. Sprinkle with the nutmeg and cook on low for about 6 hours until set. Serve with cherries and choc sprinkles on top or fruit and cream, yoghurt or ice cream. For a twist make it into a bread and butter pudding...in the next recipe.

Bread & Butter Date Pudding

Ingredients: As in recipe above:

- 4 large eggs
- 1 1/2 cups full cream milk
- 1/4 cup sugar
- 1 tsp vanilla extract
- 1/4 tsp of ground nutmeg

Add the following:

- 4 slices of white bread, buttered and with the crusts removed
- 1/2 cup chopped dates or sultana grapes

Directions:

Grease the crock pot dish with butter or oil. In a bowl, beat the eggs, sugar, milk and vanilla extract together until well combined. Pour into the crock pot. Sprinkle with the nutmeg and cook on low for about 6 hours until set. Serve with fruit and cream, yoghurt or ice cream. For a twist make it into a bread and butter pudding...in the next recipe.

Ginger Poached Pears

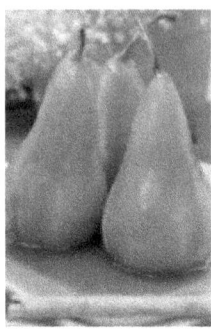

Ingredients:

4 large or 6 small firm cooking pears, peeled, cored and halved (or whole)
1/2 cup rum (can use fruit liqueur like cherry etc)
3 cups good quality apple juice
1 fresh cinnamon stick
2 tsp chopped crystallized ginger
1 quartered lemon

Directions:

In a bowl or saucepan, combine the rum, apple juice and ginger. Place the pears in the crock pot. Pour mixture over the top. Add the cinnamon stick and place the lemon pieces over the top of the pears. Cook on low for about 3 hours, or till pears are cooked (longer if whole) Remove the cinnamon and lemon, pour sauce over pears to serve. Serve with cream or vanilla ice cream.

Part 2

Introduction

I cook because I love to cook. This is my passion and I cannot live without cooking. All this goes from childhood when I lived with my parents. I remember my mother always cooked various delicious dishes using many devices. Slow Cooker was one of these kitchen appliances that helped mom create superb meals for the whole family.

A lot of time has passed since that moment. Now I'm living separately for a long time, but my love for cooking only grew from year to year. Slow Cooker became one of my favorite kitchen appliances. The key advantage of this device is that I can cook healthy and delicious dishes without spending time on it. I just need to load needed ingredients according to the chosen recipe, choose the necessary program and continue to do your own household chores. Moreover, I can even turn on my Slow Cooker in the morning and go to work. And in the evening, me and my family will receive a delicious and hot dinner from my favorite Slow Cooker!

In this cookbook you will find a great variety of recipes for all occasions. You will get recipes for healthy and hearty breakfasts, excellent snacks for large companies, meat and poultry dishes, vegetable recipes and even desserts. All that you lacked in your other cookbooks you can find in HERE!

Slow Food – Good Food

Preparing your favorite meals with the help of Slow Cocker is becoming more popular. Of course, each of us has his own favorite devices and favorite recipes, but Slow Cooker also has many advantages that will allow you to look at this kitchen device in a different way.

Slow Cooker helps to prepare delicious dishes for hundreds years and with it's help you can cook almost anything: breakfasts, side dishes, courses, meat and vegetable dishes, desserts.

6 Benefits of Slow Cooking

There are numerous reasons to love Slow Cooker. Here are just a few of the main advantages, however, the more you'll use this device in the kitchen, this list will increase.

Time-saver device
From now you are not a slave in your kitchen. All time you need is only for preparation, no more than 10-15 minutes. Your slow cooker will do all the job while you are doing anything else.

One-pot dishes
You can cook your favorite dishes without a lot of dishes for washing. Slow cooker is the perfect device for one-pot dishes. Just load prepared ingredients, turn on the device and that's all!

Delicious & healthy dishes
Since preparing in the slow cooker is mainly using fresh ingredients, a low cooking temperature leaves a numerous useful components. Vegetables and meat cooked in the slow cooker give off a lot of juices, soak them up, mix, giving a fuller flavor.

Easy cleaning
Thanks to the fact that only one device is used, washing it is much easier and faster than a huge number of pans, pots and other appliances.

Usage all year round
Slow cooker is the ideal device for cooking vegetables. Therefore it is perfect for cooking dishes from summer

vegetables such as zucchini, broccoli, tomatoes and peppers, and from winter ones - pumpkin, carrots, potatoes and so on.

Eco-friendly
Due to the fact that cooking temperature is significantly reduced, you use less energy. Thus, cooking in the slow cooker is an eco friendly and allows you to use two times less energy.

Cooking Measurement Conversion Chart

Liquid Measures

1 gal = 4 qt = 8 pt = 16 cups = 128 fl oz
½ gal = 2 qt = 4 pt = 8 cups = 64 fl oz
¼ gal = 1 qt = 2 pt = 4 cups = 32 fl oz
½ qt = 1 pt = 2 cups = 16 fl oz
¼ qt = ½ pt = 1 cup = 8 fl oz

Dry Measures

1 cup = 16 Tbsp = 48 tsp = 250ml
¾ cup = 12 Tbsp = 36 tsp = 175ml
⅔ cup = 10 ⅔ Tbsp = 32 tsp = 150ml
½ cup = 8 Tbsp = 24 tsp = 125ml
⅓ cup = 5 ⅓ Tbsp = 16 tsp = 75ml
¼ cup = 4 Tbsp = 12 tsp = 50ml
⅛ cup = 2 Tbsp = 6 tsp = 30ml
1 Tbsp = 3 tsp = 15ml

Dash or Pinch or Speck = less than ⅛ tsp

Quickies

1 fl oz = 30 ml
1 oz = 28.35 g
1 lb = 16 oz (454 g)
1 kg = 2.2 lb
1 quart = 2 pints

U.S.	Canadian
¼ tsp	1.25 mL
½ tsp	2.5 mL
1 tsp	5 mL
1 Tbl	15 mL
¼ cup	50 mL
⅓ cup	75 mL
½ cup	125 mL
⅔ cup	150 mL
¾ cup	175 mL
1 cup	250 mL
1 quart	1 liter

Recipe Abbreviations

Cup = c or C
Fluid = fl
Gallon = gal
Ounce = oz
Package = pkg
Pint = pt
Pound = lb or #
Quart = qt
Square = sq
Tablespoon = T or Tbl or TBSP or TBS
Teaspoon = t or tsp

Fahrenheit (°F) to Celcius (°C)
°C = (°F - 32) x 5/9

Fahrenheit	Celcius
32°F	0°C
40°F	4°C
140°F	60°C
150°F	65°C
160°F	70°C
225°F	107°C
250°F	121°C
275°F	135°C
300°F	150°C
325°F	165°C
350°F	177°C
375°F	190°C
400°F	205°C
425°F	220°C
450°F	230°C
475°F	245°C
500°F	260°C

OVEN TEMPERATURES

WARMING: 200°F
VERY SLOW: 250°F - 275°F
SLOW: 300°F - 325°F
MODERATE: 350°F - 375°F
HOT: 400°F - 425°F
VERY HOT: 450°F - 475°F

*Some measurements were rounded

Optimize your Metabolism

Optimizing metabolism is a main key to weight loss. It means that you will burn more calories even when you're rest, even without physical workout. Here's useful chart with 12 main foods which will boost your metabolism. Just include as many of these products as you can in your daily diet and get a great opportunity to control your weight and create a perfect body!

12 FOODS THAT BOOST YOUR METABOLISM!

Grapefruit	Yogurt	Almonds
Green Tea	Apples	Oatmeal
Broccoli	Spinach	Turkey
Jalapeno	Coffee	Cinnamon

Weight Loss Diet Tips that Really Work

Please also check main weight loss tips which can help you control body weight.

Healthy Breakfast Recipes

Healthy Overnight Steel Cut Oats

Prep time: 12 minutes, cook time: 6-7 hours, ingredients: 5-6

Ingredients

- 1 - ½ cups frozen blueberries (or another berries on your preference)
- 2 cups water
- 1 cup skimmed milk
- 1 large banana, mashed
- 1 cup steel cut oats
- 1 teaspoon ground cinnamon
- 1 tablespoon sugar (optional)
- Honey for serving

Directions

1. Pour in water and milk in a slow cooker.
2. Add mashed banana, frozen berries, and steel cut oats. Season with ground cinnamon.
3. Cover and cook on high for about 1 hour. When timer beeps, switch to "warm" and cook overnight (for about 6-8 hours).
4. Serve with honey or sugar.

Appetizing Chicken Caesar Sandwich

Prep time: 10 minutes, cook time: 4-5 hours, servings: 4-6

Ingredients

- 2 pounds chicken breasts, boneless and skinless
- ½ cup Caesar dressing
- ½ cup parmesan cheese, shredded
- ¼ cup fresh parsley, chopped
- ½ teaspoon ground pepper
- 2 cups romaine lettuce, shredded
- 4-6 regular size hamburger buns

Preparation

1. Put chicken breasts into the slow cooker, pour 1-2 cups of water over, cover and cook on low for 4-5 hours.
2. Remove cooked chicken from the Crockpot, drain the water from the slow cooker.
3. Shred the chicken using two forks and discarding any fat.
4. Place shredded chicken back to the slow cooker and pour dressing, parmesan cheese, parsley and pepper over.
5. Stir evenly.
6. Cover and cook for another 30 minutes or until ready.

7. Spoon the mixture into each slider bun.
8. Top with extra parmesan cheese and lettuce and serve.

Breakfast Sausage Scramble

Prep time: 10 minutes, cook time: 3 hours, servings: 4-6

Ingredients

- 1 pound Italian sausage
- 1 large onion, diced
- 1 garlic clove, minced
- 4 large potatoes, peeled and diced
- 1 large tomato, diced
- 1 cup frozen kernel corn
- 2 tablespoons freshly chopped parsley
- 1 - ½ cups Cheddar cheese, grated

Directions

1. In the large skillet sauté diced onion over medium-high heat for about 4-5 minutes. Add sausage and scramble.
2. Transfer cooked sausage with onions to a slow cooker basket. Add garlic, potatoes, tomatoes, frozen corn, chopped parsley, and cheese.
3. Cover and cook on low for 5-6 hours.

Asian Style Chicken Congee

Prep time: 2 minutes, cook time: 5 hours, servings: 6

Ingredients

- 6 medium chicken thighs
- 2 cups uncooked rice
- 8-10 ginger slices
- 8 cups water
- 1 tablespoon salt
- ½ teaspoon black pepper
- Soya sauce and chopped green onion for garnish (optional)

Directions

1. Add chicken thighs to your crock pot and season with salt generously. Cover thighs with rice add ginger, more salt and pepper. Pour in water and close the lid.
2. Cook on high for 5 hours.
3. When ready, open the lid and discard ginger and stir to combine.

Serve hot congee to plates and top with soya sauce or chopped green onions

Delicious Oatmeal with Apples

Prep time: 10 minutes, cook time: 4-5 hours, servings: 4-5

Ingredients

- 1 tablespoon butter
- 1 cup dried oatmeal
- 1 large apple, peeled and sliced
- 2 cups milk
- 1-2 tablespoons honey
- A pinch of salt
- Brown sugar and nuts for garnish

Directions

1. Add oatmeal, sliced apple, milk, honey, and salt in a large bowl. Stir to combine.
2. Grease a slow cooker with butter and pour in prepared mixture.
3. Cover and cook on high for 4 hours.
4. Serve into individual plates and garnish with brown sugar and nuts.

Delicious Morning Pudding with Dried Figs

Prep time: 5 minutes, cook time: 3 hours, servings: 6

Ingredients

- 4 cups bread cubes
- 4 large eggs
- 1 cup skim milk
- 3 tablespoon melted butter
- ½ tablespoon sugar
- ¼ teaspoon ground cinnamon
- ¼ teaspoon ground cloves
- ½ cup dried figs, cut

Directions

1. Cut bread into 1-inch cubes and transfer to a slow cooker.
2. In the mixing bowl combine milk, eggs, melted butter, sugar, cinnamon and cloves. Stir to combine.
3. Pour the mixture to a slow cooker pot over bread cubes.
4. Close the lid and cook on low for 3 hours.

Amazing French Toast Casserole

Prep time: 5 minutes, cook time: 6 hours, servings: 8

Ingredients

- ½ pound bread, cut into 1-inch cubes
- 6 large eggs
- 1 cup whole milk
- 1 teaspoon almond extract
- 1 cup of half and half
- 1 teaspoon of lemon zest, grated
- ¼ teaspoon ground cloves
- ¼ teaspoon ground cinnamon
- ½ teaspoon vanilla extract
- 3 tablespoons sugar
- 1 cup almonds

Directions

1. Preheat the oven for 230 F and bake bread cubes for 30 minutes, until become crunchy.
2. Place bread cubes on the bottom of slow cooker pot.
3. In the medium bowl combine lemon zest, eggs, almond extract, half and half, cinnamon, ground cloves. Mix well and pour the mixture in a slow cooker. Top with almonds and cook on low for 4-5 hours.
4. When ready serve with honey or maple syrup.

Steel-Cut Oats with Honey

Prep time: 2 minutes, cook time: 3-4 hours, servings: 6

Ingredients

- 1 cup steel-cut oatmeal
- 1 cup skimmed milk
- 2 cups water
- 4 tablespoons almond butter
- 5-6 tablespoons honey
- Salt, to taste

Directions

1. In a large bowl combine water, milk and steel-cut oatmeal. Season with salt and mix well.
2. Transfer the mixture to a slow cooker, close the lid and cook in high for 3-4 hours.
3. When ready, stir in almond butter, top with honey and serve.

Breakfast Pumpkin Bread with Cranberries

Prep time: 5 minutes, cook time: 2 hours, servings: 8

Ingredients

- ¾ cup canned pumpkin
- ½ cup half and half
- 2 tablespoons sugar
- ½ cup frozen or fresh cranberries
- 1 teaspoon ground cinnamon
- ¼ teaspoon ground cardamom
- 2 cups all-purpose flour
- 1 teaspoon baking soda
- 1 teaspoon baking powder
- A pinch of salt to taste
- ¼ cup unsalted butter
- ½ cup roasted peanuts, chopped

Directions

1. In the mixing bowl combine sugar, ground spices, and half and half cream.
2. In another bowl mix all-purpose flour, baking soda, baking powder and salt, to taste.
3. Add butter and canned pumpkin to the mixture. Stir to combine.
4. Add cranberries and mix again.
5. Spoon the batter into the slow cooker. Scatter chopped peanuts on the top and cook on low for 2 hours.

6. When ready, serve and enjoy.

Omelette Casserole

Prep time: 15 minutes, cook time: 4 hours, servings: 4

Ingredients
- ½ pound sausage on your preference or cooked ham
- 7 large eggs
- 1 cup whole milk
- 1 pound frozen hash brown potatoes
- 1 medium onion, chopped
- 1 small bell pepper, chopped
- ½ cup shredded cheese
- Salt and pepper, to taste

Directions

1. Lay on the bottom of the crock pot the half of ham or sausage. Add 1/2 frozen hash brown potatoes, then onions, peppers. Season with salt and pepper. Cover with half of shredded cheese.
2. Repeat layers.
3. In the mixing bowl combine beaten eggs with milk. Whisk well. Add salt and pepper, to taste.
4. Pour the mixture over the casserole to a slow cooker and cover the lid.
5. Cook on low for 3-4 hours.
6. Garnish with chopped parsley or dill and serve hot.

Pumpkin Spice Clean Eating Pot Oatmeal

Prep time: 15 minutes, cook time: 4 hours, servings: 8

Ingredients

- 2 cups of steel cut oats
- 1 can (15 oz) pumpkin puree
- 1 tablespoon softened butter
- 4 cups water
- 1 cup milk
- ¼ cup maple syrup
- 2 tablespoons brown sugar
- 1 tablespoon vanilla
- ¼ teaspoon cinnamon

Directions

1. Grease the slow cooker pot with butter.
2. In the large bowl combine all ingredients, including steel cut oats, water, milk, maple syrup, sugar, vanilla and cinnamon. Whisk evenly.
3. Pour the mixture to a slow cooker, close the lid and cook on low for 4 hours.
4. Serve and enjoy.

Homemade Granola

Prep time: 2 minutes, cook time: 3 hours, servings: 6

Ingredients

- 2 cups steel cut oatmeal
- ½ cup almonds, crushed
- 2 tablespoons sugar
- ¼ teaspoon ground cinnamon
- 2 tablespoons extra virgin olive oil
- 3 tablespoons honey
- 2 tablespoons dried fruits (raisins, figs), chopped
- A dash of salt, to taste

Directions

1. Sprinkle the slow cooker pot with olive oil.
2. Add oatmeal, cinnamon, and sugar to a slow cooker. Season with salt and stir to combine.
3. Add honey and mix well.
4. Cook on low for 3 hours. In order to make granola crunchy, close the lid partially to make the air and extra moisture escape.
5. When ready stir in chopped dried fruits and serve.

Homemade Greek Yogurt

Prep time: 5 minutes, cook time: 7 hours, servings: 8

Ingredients

- 16 cups whole milk
- 1 cup plain yogurt (must have live cultures)

Directions

1. Add whole milk to your crock pot. Close the lid and cook on high for 2-3 hours.
2. Open the lid and using thermometer check the temperature. It need to be not more than 110 F. If milk is hot set aside to chill.
3. When temperature is OK, stir in plain yogurt, mix well and close the lid. Wrap crock pot with a warm kitchen towel and set aside for 8 hours.
4. Open the lid and ladle your Greek yogurt to a plate. You may use any topping you like: nuts, honey, cinnamon, brown sugar or anything else.

Banana Oatmeal

Prep time: 5 minutes, cook time: 4 hours, servings: 5-6

Ingredients

- 1 cup of steel cut oats
- 2 middle-sized ripped bananas, mashed
- 3 tablespoons sugar
- ¼ teaspoon vanilla
- A pinch of cinnamon
- ½ cup roasted pecans
- Salt to taste

Directions

1. Add ripped bananas to a large bowl and mash them up. Pour in milk, add cinnamon, sugar, vanilla, oats. Season with salt. Stir to combine well.
2. Transfer the mixture to a slow cooker, close the lid and cook on high for 4-5 hours.
3. Once ready, carefully open the lid, serve and top with roasted pecans.

Italian Spicy Omelette

Prep time: 5 minutes, cook time: 2 hours, servings: 4

Ingredients

- 5-6 large eggs
- 1 cup cauliflower, cut into florets
- 1 cup skim milk
- ½ cup shredded Cheddar cheese
- ½ teaspoon dried basil
- ½ teaspoon dried oregano
- ½ teaspoon dried parsley
- ½ teaspoon dried dill
- ¼ teaspoon black pepper
- 2 small garlic cloves, minced
- A pinch of chili powder
- 1 tablespoon olive oil

Directions

1. Drizzle the crock pot with olive oil.
2. In the large mixing bowl combine milk, eggs and spices. Mix well. Then, stir in cauliflower florets, garlic cloves and 1/2 of cheese.
3. Pour the mixture to a slow cooker and close the lid. Cook for 2 hours on slow.
4. When ready, serve the omelette into plates and top with the remaining cheese.
5. Enjoy.

Delicious Vegetable and Bacon Quiche

Prep time: 5 minutes, cook time: 4 hours, servings: 4

Ingredients

- 4 slices bacon
- 1 cup spinach
- 1 small onion, chopped
- 2 cups whole milk
- 8 large sized eggs
- 2 garlic cloves, minced
- 1 teaspoon dried basil
- 1 cup Cheddar cheese, grated
- 1 medium bell pepper, chopped
- ½ teaspoon salt
- ¼ teaspoon black pepper
- 1 tablespoon olive oil

Directions

1. Cook bacon slices in the skillet over medium-high heat for 3-5 minutes, until crispy.
2. In the same skillet add olive oil and cook chopped bell pepper, onions, spinach and garlic for 5 minutes. Set aside.
3. In the mixing bowl combine eggs, milk, grated cheese and season with salt and pepper. Mix well.
4. In a slow cooker add vegetable mixture, add bacon slices and pour egg mixture over it. Season with salt

and pepper lightly and close the lid. Cook on low for 4 hours.
5. Serve and enjoy.

Morning Oatmeal with Dried Fruits

Prep time: 5 minutes, cook time: 8 hours, servings: 6

Ingredients

- 2 cups steel cut oats
- 1/2 cup dried berries
- ½ cup raisins
- ½ cup dried figs
- 1 tablespoon brown sugar
- 3 cups water
- 1 cup whole milk

Directions

1. Combine all ingredients in the slow cooker pot. Stir well and pour in water.
2. Close the lid and cook overnight on low for 8 hours.
3. Serve in the morning and get valuable and healthy breakfast!

Delicious Breakfast Hash Brown

Prep time: 10 minutes, cook time: 6 hours, servings: 10

Ingredients

- 1 pound cooked ham
- 1 bag frozen hash browns
- 4 garlic cloves, minced
- 1 medium sized onion, diced
- 1 cup shredded cheese
- 1 cup skim milk
- 10 large eggs
- ½ teaspoon salt
- ¼ teaspoon black pepper.
- ½ teaspoon dried thyme

Directions

1. Add ingredients to a slow cooker pot in the following order: 1/2 hash browns, 1/2 cooked ham, 1/2 onions 1/2 cheese. Then repeat layers in the same order.
2. In the mixing bowl combine milk, eggs, season with salt, pepper and thyme.
3. Pour the mixture into the crock pot and cook for 5-6 hours.
4. Serve and enjoy.

Easy Potato Breakfast

Prep time: 10 minutes, cook time: 3-4 hours, servings: 6-7

Ingredients

- 1 - ½ pounds frozen hash brown potatoes, defrosted
- 1 pound minced beef
- 10 eggs, beaten
- ½ cup milk
- 2 cups shredded cheese
- 1 tablespoon olive oil
- ½ teaspoon salt
- ¼ teaspoon black pepper

Directions

1. Preheat olive oil in a large skillet over medium-high heat and brown minced beef for about 7-10 minutes, stirring occasionally. Add salt and pepper to taste.
2. Meanwhile, beat eggs in a mixing bowl.
3. Place defrosted potatoes to a slow cooker basket and season with salt and pepper.
4. Cover with cooked meat, pour in eggs and milk and sprinkle with shredded cheese.
5. Cook on low for 3-4 hours.
6. Serve hot and enjoy!

Savory Appetizers

Delicious Parmesan-Crusted Chicken

Prep time: 10 minutes, cook time: 4-5 hours, servings: 5

Ingredients

- 2-3 chicken breasts, skinless
- ½ cup Italian seasoned breadcrumbs
- ¼ cup parmesan cheese, grated
- ¼ teaspoon ground black pepper
- ¼ teaspoon salt
- 1 tablespoon Olive oil
- 1 egg, beaten
- Sliced mozzarella cheese (optional)
- Favorite marinara sauce

Directions

1. Sprinkle 1 tablespoon of olive oil on the bottom of the slow cooker.
2. In a small bowl whisk the egg.
3. Mix Italian seasoned breadcrumbs, parmesan, ground pepper and salt in the middle bowl.
4. Dip the chicken into the egg and then into the breadcrumbs mixture. Evenly cover all sides of the chicken with egg and mixture.
5. Put the chicken breasts in the bottom of the crock pot.
6. Lay 3-4 slices of mozzarella cheese on top (optional).

7. Pour your favorite marinara sauce over chicken and cheese.
8. Close lid and prepare for low for 4-5 hours or until chicken becomes ready.
9. Serve with rice or pasta.

Crock Pot Cheese Fondue

Prep time: 10 minutes, cook time: 2 hours, servings: 3-4

Ingredients

- 1 tablespoon butter
- 1 small onion, chopped
- 1 garlic clove, minced
- 1 tablespoon all-purpose flour
- 5-6 tablespoons dry white wine
- 4 tablespoons skimmed milk
- ½ cup shredded Cheddar cheese
- ½ cup Gruyere cheese
- 2 oz Blue cheese

Directions

1. Add all ingredients to a large bowl. Pour in wine and milk and stir to combine.
2. Transfer the mixture to a slow cooker, cover and cook on low for 3-4 hours stirring couple time while cooking, until cheese melted.

Mexican Style Chili Colorado Burritos

Prep time: 12 minutes, cook time: 6 hours, servings: 4-6

Ingredients

- 1 ½ pound stew meat (beef)
- 1 can (18 oz) red enchilada sauce
- 2 beef bouillon cubes
- 1 can beans
- 6-8 burrito size tortillas
- 1 cup cheese (or more, depends on your preference), shredded

Directions

1. Cut beef into small pieces and put into the slow cooker.
2. Crush bouillon cubes over beef and add enchilada sauce.
3. Cook on low for at least 6 hours or until beef is very tender.
4. When meat is done, season to taste with salt and pepper.
5. Warm up beans.
6. Put couple teaspoons of beans in the center of each tortilla.
7. Add about ½ cup of beef and roll into a burrito.
8. Place burritos into a greased baking pan. Pour some extra sauce over the tops of the burritos to cover them. Place cheese on top.
9. Roast until cheese golden, maybe 2-4 minutes.

Slow Cooker Chicken Wings

Prep time: 10 minutes, cook time: 3 - 1/2 hours, servings: 4-6

Ingredients

- 2 pounds chicken wings
- 3 tablespoons freshly squeezed lemon juice
- 4 tablespoons honey
- ¼ cup water
- ½ tablespoon garlic powder
- ½ teaspoon ground ginger
- Salt and pepper, to taste

Directions

1. Mix honey, lemon juice, water, garlic powder, ground ginger, salt and pepper in a bowl.
2. Place chicken wings to a slow cooker. Pour honey mixture over wings and stir to combine.
3. Cover and cook on high for 3-4 hours, until cooked and tender.
4. Serve and enjoy.

Simple BBQ Ribs

Prep time: 8 minutes, cook time: 6-8 hours, servings: 6

Ingredients

- 3 pounds pork loin ribs, boneless
- 3 tablespoon liquid smoke
- ½ cup brown sugar
- ½ cup sweet onion, diced
- 1 bottle (18 oz) favorite BBQ sauce

Directions

1. Cover slow cooker with cooking spray.
2. Rub pork ribs with liquid smoke. Place them into the slow cooker.
3. Sprinkle brown sugar over the top of the ribs.
4. Pour the bottle of your favorite BBQ sauce over the of the ribs.
5. Cover and cook on low for 6-8 hours until ribs become tender.

Classic Beef Lasagna

Prep time: 10 minutes, cook time: 4-6 hours, servings: 5-7

Ingredients

- 1 ground pound beef
- 1 jar (24 oz) Traditional Pasta Sauce
- 1 cup water
- 15 oz Original Ricotta Cheese
- 7 oz 2% milk shredded mozzarella cheese, divided
- ¼ cup parmesan cheese, grated and divided
- 1 egg
- 2 tablespoon fresh parsley, chopped
- 6 lasagna noodles, uncooked

Directions

1. Brown ground beef a little in a large skillet, drain.
2. Stir in pasta sauce and water.
3. Combine 1 ½ cups ricotta, 2 tablespoon parmesan, egg and chopped parsley.
4. Put 1 cup meat mixture into the slow cooker, top with noodles (broken) and cheese mixture. Cover with 2 cups of meat mixture. Top with remaining noodles (broken), cheese and meat sauce.
5. Cover with lid and cook on low 4-6 hours, until liquid absorbed.
6. Then open, sprinkle with remaining cheeses and let stand covered up to 10 minutes until melted.

Broccoli & Bacon Cheesy Appetizer

Prep time: 15 minutes, cook time: 2 hours, servings: 10-12

Ingredients

- 1 can (10 oz) mushroom soup
- 14 slices cooked bacon
- 1 pound broccoli, cut into florets, and blanched
- 2 - ½ cups shredded Cheddar cheese
- 1/3 cup water
- 1 teaspoon mustard

Directions

1. Mix together canned soup, mustard, and water.
2. Place cooked bacon, blanched broccoli and shredded cheese into a slow cooker and pour the soup mixture over. Stir to combine well.
3. Cook on high for 1-2 hours and serve hot.

Crock Pot Chipotle Chili

Prep time: 15 minutes, cook time: 5 hours, servings: 5-6

Ingredients

- 1 - ½ pounds ground beef
- 1 large onion, diced
- 3 garlic cloves, minced
- 1 can (14 fl oz) black beans
- 1 can (14 fl oz) kidney beans
- 1 can (14 fl oz) pinto beans
- 2 cans (15 fl oz each) diced tomatoes
- 1 small can chipotle chilies in adobe sauce
- 2 teaspoons chili powder
- 1 teaspoon ground cumin
- ½ teaspoon salt
- ¼ teaspoon black pepper

Directions

1. Brown ground beef in a large skillet until no longer pink, for about 6-8 minutes. Transfer meat to a slow cooker basket.
2. Add onions and garlic on top.
3. Drain and rinse beans and also add them to a slow cooker. Add tomatoes and spices.
4. Cover and cook on high for 5 hours.
5. Sprinkle with freshly chopped parsley or dill (optional) and serve hot.

Crispy Chicken Taquitos

Prep time: 10 minutes, cook time: 3 hours, servings: 6

Ingredients

- 3 large chicken breasts, skinless and boneless
- ½ cup water
- 1 cup cream cheese
- 1 cup Mexican blend cheese
- 3 jalapenos, chopped
- 1 teaspoon onion powder
- 1 teaspoon garlic powder
- ½ teaspoon salt
- 12 taco flour tortillas

Directions

1. Place the chicken breasts to a slow cooker. Add cream cheese, water, onion and garlic powders. Season with salt, to taste. Close the lid and cook on high for 4-5 hours.
2. Open the lid and remove chicken breasts. Shred meat with two forks and transfer to a slow cooker. Stir to combine.
3. Meanwhile, heat up flour tortillas in the microwave to soften them.
4. Spread the Mexican blend cheese on each tortilla and top with chicken mixture from a slow cooker.
5. Roll up stuffed tortilla and serve hot. Enjoy.

Mashed Potatoes

Prep time: 20 minutes, cook time: 4 hours, servings: 4

Ingredients

- 2 pounds potatoes, peeled and diced
- 4 tablespoons butter
- 1/2 cup chicken stock
- ½ cup milk
- 1 teaspoon salt
- ½ teaspoon black pepper
- 3 tablespoons Parmesan cheese, grated

Directions

1. Peel and dice potatoes, and transfer to a slow cooker. Add butter and chicken stock. Season with salt and pepper. Close the lid and cook on low for 4 hours.
2. When potatoes become tender, mash it including all juices and adding milk and grated Parmesan cheese. Add needed milk quantity to achieve desired consistency.
3. Serve and enjoy.

Butternut Squash Risotto with Goat Cheese

Prep time: 15 minutes, cook time: 6 hours, servings: 4

Ingredients

- 2 pounds butternut squash, peeled and cut into 1-inch pieces
- ¼ cup shallots, finely chopped
- ¼ cup dry white wine
- 2 cups chicken or vegetable stock
- 1 cup brown rice, uncooked
- ¾ cup goat cheese, crumbled
- 1 teaspoon olive oil
- ½ teaspoon salt
- ¼ teaspoon black pepper
- Fresh sage leaves (for garnish), chopped

Directions

1. Grease the crock pot with olive oil. Add chopped shallots and cook for 4 minutes using Sauté mode. Add butternut squash cut into 1-inch cubes, rice and pour in chicken or vegetable stock.
2. Close the lid and cook on low for 5-6 hours until rice cooked.
3. Stir in crumbled cheese.
4. Top with fresh sage leaves and serve.

Amazing Mexican Queso Fundid

Prep time: 5 minutes, cook time: 2 hours, servings: 5-6

Ingredients

- 12 warm corn tortillas
- 1 cup low-fat cheese
- 1 cup sharp cheese, shredded
- 2/3 cup skimmed milk
- 1 cup chorizo sausage, chopped
- 1 small roasted red pepper
- 1 tablespoon pickled jalapeno peppers
- Chopped cilantro and dill for garnish

Directions

1. Mix all ingredients excluding sausages and roast pepper in your slow cooker pot and cook for 20 minutes on high until cheese completely melted.
2. Add sausage and roast red pepper, stir well. Cover the lid and cook for another 1 hour 30 minutes.
3. When ready, divide the mixture among corn tortillas. Sprinkle with chopped herbs and serve.

Green Bean Casserole

Prep time: 13 minutes, cook time: 3 hours, servings: 4-6

Ingredients

- 2 can (15 oz) cut green beans, drained
- 1 can (10 oz) cream of mushroom soup, undiluted
- 1 package (8 oz) Cheddar cheese, shredded
- 5 oz fresh mushrooms, drained and sliced
- 1 cup milk
- 1 tablespoon Worcestershire sauce
- 1 can (6 oz) French fried onion rings, divided
- 1 teaspoon ground pepper
- Salt to taste

Directions

1. In the large bowl combine green beans, mushroom soup, cheddar cheese, fresh mushrooms, milk, sauce and pepper.
2. Stir in half of French fried onion rings.
3. Grace slow cooker lightly and put casserole mixture into the crockpot.
4. Cover and cook on low for 2 hours.
5. Sprinkle remaining onion rings on the top of the dish, cover and cook another 30-40 minutes.
6. Serve and enjoy.

Slow Cooker BBQ Chicken

Prep time: 6 minutes, cook time: 6 hours, servings: 4

Ingredients

- 1 ½ pounds chicken breasts, boneless and skinless
- 1 bottle favorite BBQ Sauce
- ¼ cup vinegar
- 1 teaspoon red pepper flakes
- 1 tablespoon brown sugar
- 1 teaspoon garlic powder

Directions

1. Prepare chicken breasts.
2. In the middle bowl combine BBQ sauce, vinegar, red pepper flakes, brown sugar and garlic powder.
3. Place prepared chicken breasts to the slow cooker and pour the mixture over.
4. Cover and cook on low for 5-6 hours.
5. Enjoy!

Easy Main Dishes

Potatoes with Bacon & Beans

Prep time: 15 minutes, cook time: 6 hours, servings: 8

Ingredients

- 7-8 bacon strips, chopped
- 1 pound fresh green beans, cut into 2-inch pieces
- ½ pound potatoes, peeled and cut into 1/2-inch cubes
- 1 medium onion, sliced
- ¼ cup chicken stock
- Salt and pepper, to taste

Directions

1. Cook chopped bacon in the skillet over medium heat, until crisp, for about 4-5 minutes.
2. Remove bacon to kitchen towels, dry and set aside until serving.
3. Mix chopped beans, potatoes, and onions in your crock pot. Pour in chicken stock and couple tablespoons grease from the skillet. Season with salt and pepper, to taste, cover and cook on low for 6 hours until potatoes are cooked and tender.
4. Add bacon, stir to combine and serve warm.

Tender Beef and Broccoli

Prep time: 6 minutes, cook time: 6 hours, servings: 5-6

Ingredients

- 1 pound beef chuck roast, sliced
- 1 cup beef broth
- ½ cup soy sauce
- 1/3 cup brown sugar
- 1 tablespoon sesame oil
- 3 garlic cloves, minced
- 2 tablespoons cornstarch
- 2 tablespoons water
- Fresh broccoli (as many as you like)
- Cooked rice

Directions

1. Slice beef into thin strips.
2. Place meat in a slow cooker.
3. In a middle bowl mix broth, soy sauce, brown sugar, sesame oil and garlic. Pour over beef.
4. Cover and cook on low for 6 hours.
5. In a little bowl stir cornstarch with water until smooth. Add to a slow cooker. Mix well.
6. Blanch broccoli and add to the crockpot. Stir to combine.
7. Cover and cook additionally for 20-25 minutes on high.
8. Serve with hot cooked rice.

Pork Roast in Mustard Sauce

Prep time: 15 minutes, cook time: 4-4,5 hours, servings: 4-5

Ingredients

- 2-3 pound pork loin
- 2 tablespoons Italian seasoning
- 1 can (14 oz) cranberry sauce
- 3 tablespoons Dijon mustard
- 2 tablespoons olive oil
- Salt, to taste

Directions

1. Heat the olive oil in a large skillet. Brown pork roast from all sides for about 3-4 minutes.
2. Transfer meat to a slow cooker and season with salt and Italian seasoning. Pour in cranberry sauce and cover the cooker.
3. Cook on low for 4 hours until meat is tender. Remove pork roast to a plate.
4. Stir mustard into cooking juices.
5. Slice the pork loin and serve with cranberry-mustard sauce.

Sweet Potato Stew with Chicken

Prep time: 15 minutes, cook time: 4 hours, servings: 6-7

Ingredients

- 2 pounds chicken breasts, cubed
- 4 large sweet potatoes, peeled and cut into cubes
- 2 yellow potatoes, peeled and cubed
- 3 large carrots, sliced
- 2 cups chicken or vegetable stock
- 2 cans (15 fl oz each) tomatoes
- 2 teaspoons smoked paprika
- ½ teaspoon ground cumin
- 3 tablespoons fresh basil
- Salt and black pepper, to taste

Directions

1. Cut chicken breasts into 1-inch cubes and transfer to a slow cooker basket.
2. Do the same with potatoes. Add sliced carrots and tomatoes. Pour in stock and season with salt, pepper, and other spices. Stir to combine well.
3. Cover and cook on high for 4-5 hours or until meat become ready and tender.
4. Serve hot.

Outstanding Sweet Pork

Prep time: 10 minutes, cook time: 4 hours, servings: 5-6

Ingredients

- 2 pounds pork
- 2 cans Coke (not diet)
- 1 teaspoon garlic salt
- ½ cup brown sugar
- ¼ cup water
- 1 can (4 oz) green chilies, diced
- 1 can (10 oz) enchilada sauce

Directions

1. Take a large zip-lock bag and place the pork into it.
2. Add there 1 can of Coke, ½ cup of brown sugar. Make sure the pork dips into the marinade. Place the bag in the fridge for the whole night.
3. After that drain the marinade and put pork into the slow cooker.
4. Add ½ can of Coke, water and garlic salt over the meat.
5. Cook on high for at least 3-4 hours.
6. Once meat is almost ready shred it up with 2 forks.
7. Mix remaining Coke, green chilies, enchilada sauce and sugar in the large bowl.
8. Serve the pork with sauce and enjoy!

Delicious Pork Stew

Prep time: 10 minutes, cook time: 5 hours, servings: 7-8

Ingredients

- 2 pounds pork tenderloin, cut into 2-inch chunks
- 3 medium carrots, sliced
- 1 large onion, chopped
- 3 garlic cloves, chopped
- 3 cups chicken or beef stock
- 2 tablespoons tomato paste
- 1 rosemary sprig
- 1 thyme sprig
- Salt and black pepper, to taste
- Freshly chopped parsley for garnish

Directions

1. Cut pork and rub with salt and pepper. Transfer meat chunks to a slow cooker.
2. Add carrots, onions, garlic. Whisk stock and tomato paste and pour in the slow cooker pot.
3. Top with rosemary and thyme, cover and cook on low for 4-5 hours until meat is tender.
4. Discard thyme and rosemary, serve and sprinkle with freshly chopped parsley.

Your Favorite Homemade Potatoes with Pork

Prep time: 10 minutes, cook time: 6 hours, servings: 6

Ingredients

- 2 pounds pork tenderloin
- 6 large potatoes, peeled and cut into 1-inch cubes
- 2 medium onions, chopped
- 2 garlic cloves, crushed
- 1 cup vegetable or chicken stock
- ¼ cup soy sauce
- ¼ cup dry white wine
- 1 tablespoon Worcestershire sauce
- 3 tablespoons cornstarch
- 1 tablespoon olive oil
- 1 teaspoon salt
- ¼ teaspoon black pepper
- 2 tablespoons freshly chopped parsley

Directions

1. Heat the olive oil in a large skillet over medium-high heat. Brown pork tenderloin from all sides for about 4-6 minutes.
2. Mix chicken stock, soy sauce, wine, Worcestershire sauce, onions and garlic in the slow cooker basket. Whisk in cornstarch. Stir to combine well.
3. Add meat, cover the lid and cook on low for 4 hours.
4. Uncover the slow cooker and add cubed potatoes. Cook on low for 2 hours more.

5. When ready, slice meat and serve with potatoes. Top with gravy and sprinkle with freshly chopped parsley.

Honey Chicken with Sesame Seeds

Prep time: 6 minutes, cook time: 4 hours, servings: 6-7

Ingredients

- 2 ½ pounds skinless, boneless chicken breasts or thighs (as you wish)
- 1 cup honey
- ½ cup soy sauce
- 1 medium onion, diced
- 4 tablespoons ketchup or tomato sauce
- 2 tablespoons canola oil
- 2-3 cloves garlic, minced
- 4 tablespoons cornstarch dissolved in 8 tablespoons water
- ½ teaspoon salt
- ¼ teaspoon ground pepper
- Sesame seeds

Directions

1. Sprinkle slow cooker with cooking spray.
2. Season chicken with salt on both sides and place on the bottom of the slow cooker
3. In a small bowl add honey, soy sauce, onion, ketchup, oil, garlic, and mix well. Pour over chicken.
4. Cook on low for 3-4 hours or until chicken cooked.
5. Remove chicken from the cooker and leave sauce. Dissolve cornstarch in the water and pour into the slow cooker. Mix with sauce.
6. Cook sauce on high for 10-15 minutes or until slightly thickened.

7. Cut chicken into medium pieces, return to the pot and dip in a sauce before serving.
8. Season with sesame seeds and serve with cooked rice.

Creamy Potatoes with Bratwurst Sausage

Prep time: 15 minutes, cook time: 6 hours, servings: 6-8

Ingredients

- 2 pounds potatoes, peeled and cubed
- 2 pounds uncooked bratwurst sausage
- 2 cups half-and-half cream
- 1 large carrot, chopped
- 1 large onion, chopped
- 2 garlic cloves, crushed
- 1-2 celery ribs, chopped
- 1 green bell pepper, chopped
- 1/2 cup chicken stock
- 1 teaspoon dried basil
- 1 tablespoon cornstarch
- 3 tablespoons cold water
- Salt and black pepper to taste

Directions

1. Add potatoes, onions, carrot, celery, garlic and pepper to a slow cooker. Stir to combine. Top with bratwurst links.
2. Pour in chicken stock and season with salt, pepper and basil.
3. Cook on low for 6 hours until sausages are cooked.
4. Remove sausage and cut into 1-inch pieces. Add meat to the slow cooker and stir in half-and-half cream.

5. Combine cornstarch with water until smooth. Add to stew and stir well.
6. Cover and cook on high for addition 20-30 minutes until thickened and
7. Serve hot.

Delicious Pork Carnitas

Prep time: 12 minutes, cook time: 4 hours, servings: 5-6

Ingredients

- 2 pounds pork shoulder, boneless and cut into 2-inch cubes
- 2 medium onions, chopped
- 1 can (14 fl oz) diced tomatoes
- 2 Chipotle Peppers in Adobo Sauce
- 1 bottle (12 fl oz) beer
- Juice from 1 orange
- 1 teaspoon ground coriander
- 1 teaspoon ground cumin
- 1 teaspoon salt
- A pinch of black pepper
- 1 tablespoon olive oil

Directions

1. Cut pork into 2-inch pieces and place in a slow cooker. Add chopped onions and pour in beer and orange juice.
2. Cover and cook on high for 4 hours.
3. When ready remove the pork and set aside to chill.
4. Shred pork with two forks.
5. Add tomatoes, chipotle peppers, and spices to a blender and make a puree.
6. In a large skillet preheat olive oil over medium-high heat. Brown shredded pork from all sides until become crisp.

7. Serve browned pork and pour sauce over meat.

Sweet Chicken Breast with Honey

Prep time: 10 minutes, cook time: 3 hours, servings: 3-4

Ingredients

- 1 pound chicken breast, skinless
- ¼ teaspoon ground pepper
- ½ cup honey
- ¼ cup soy sauce
- ½ teaspoon salt
- 1 onion, chopped
- 1/8 cup ketchup
- 1 tablespoon vegetable oil
- 1 clove garlic, minced
- ¼ teaspoon red pepper flakes

Directions

1. Season chicken breasts in both sides with salt and pepper. Put into the slow cooker.
2. In the medium bowl mix soy sauce, honey, chopped onion, ketchup, garlic, and pepper flakes. Pour over chicken with mixture.
3. Cook on low for at least 3 hours.
4. Cut cooked chicken into bite size pieces, return to the crockpot and cover with sauce.
5. Serve with rice or noodles.

Asian Pork Chops

Prep time: 15 minutes, cook time: 3 ½ hours, servings: 4-5

Ingredients

- 4-5 pork loin chops, boneless
- 1 large onion, chopped
- 1 green bell pepper, chopped
- 2 garlic cloves, minced
- 3 tablespoons brown sugar
- ¼ cup dry white wine
- ¼ cup soy sauce
- 1 teaspoon grated ginger
- 1 tablespoon sesame oil
- 3 tablespoons sesame seeds
- 2 tablespoons cornstarch
- 3 tablespoons cold water
- Salt and pepper, to taste
- Cooked rice for serving

Directions

1. Cover pork chops with salt and pepper. Transfer to a slow cooker pot. Add chopped onions and green pepper.
2. Mix brown sugar, dry wine, soy sauce, grated ginger, sesame oil and minced garlic. Stir to combine. Pour this mixture over meat, cover and cook on low for 4 hours until meat is tender.
3. Remove cooked meat from a slow cooker. Mix cornstarch with cold water and gradually stir into a

pan. Bring to a boil and simmer for 5 minutes until thickened.
4. Serve pork with cooker rice, top with gravy and sprinkle with sesame seeds.

Slow Cooker Chicken Adobo

Prep time: 15 minutes, cook time: 6-7 hours, servings: 5-6

Ingredients

- 3 pounds chicken thighs, bone-in
- 4 garlic cloves
- 2 medium-sized onions, sliced
- 5 tablespoons soy sauce
- 4 tablespoons apple vinegar
- 1 tablespoon garlic powder
- 1-inch piece fresh ginger, sliced
- Salt and ground black pepper, to taste
- 2 tablespoons olive oil

Directions

1. Season chicken thighs with salt, pepper, and garlic powder from all sides.
2. Preheat olive oil in the large skillet. Brown chicken on both sides until skin is golden for about 5-7 minutes.
3. Add 1 tablespoon of olive oil in the slow cooker and place onion slices on the bottom.
4. Place browned chicken thighs on the top of the onions. Lay garlic cloves and sliced ginger.
5. Pour soy sauce and vinegar over chicken and season with salt and black pepper, to taste.
6. Cover and cook on low for about 7-8 hours, until chicken tender and cooked.

Famous Santa Fe Chicken

Prep time: 13 minutes, cook time: 8-10 hours, servings: 4-6

Ingredients

- 1 ½ pounds chicken breast, skinless
- 1 can (14 oz) tomatoes with green chilies, diced
- 1 can (14 oz) black beans
- 6-8 oz frozen corn
- ½ cup fresh cilantro, chopped
- 1 can (14 oz) chicken broth
- 2 shallot, chopped
- 1 teaspoon garlic powder
- 1 teaspoon onion powder
- 1 teaspoon cumin
- 1 teaspoon cayenne pepper
- Salt and pepper for seasoning

Directions

1. In the large bowl add chicken broth, beans, corn, tomatoes, cilantro, shallot, garlic and onion powders, cumin, cayenne pepper, salt, and stir to combine.
2. Place this mixture in the slow cooker.
3. Season chicken breasts and lay them on the top of other ingredients inside the crockpot.
4. Cook on low for 8-10 hours.
5. In an hour before serving remove chicken from the slow cooker and shred.

6. Return chicken into the slow cooker and stir with other ingredients.
7. Serve and season with salt and pepper to taste.

Slow Cooker Pork Chops Cacciatore

Prep time: 20 minutes, cook time: 6 hours, servings: 6-8

Ingredients

- 6 pork loin chops, bone-in
- 1 large onion, chopped
- 2 celery ribs, chopped
- 1 small carrot, chopped
- 1 ½ cup fresh mushrooms, sliced
- 2 garlic cloves, crushed
- 1 can (12 oz) diced tomatoes
- ½ cup water
- 1 teaspoon dried cilantro
- 4 cups cooked egg noodles for serving
- 1 teaspoon salt
- ¼ teaspoon black pepper

Directions

1. Rub pork chops with salt and pepper and brown them in a large skillet over high heat. Place browned pork chops to a slow cooker.
2. Add sliced mushrooms, onions, carrots, celery to a skillet and sauté for 5-7 minutes. Add garlic and cook for 1 minute more. Transfer veggies to a slow cooker pot.
3. Stir in tomatoes and water, sprinkle with dried cilantro, add salt and pepper if desired.
4. Cover and cook on low for 6 hours or until cooked.
5. Serve the meat with cooked egg noodles and enjoy.

Tender Pork with Herb Vegetables

Prep time: 15 minutes, cook time: 4 hours, servings: 5-6

Ingredients

- 2 pounds pork tenderloin
- 1 large carrot, chopped
- 1 medium onion, chopped
- 3 large potatoes, do not peeled
- 3 garlic cloves, minced
- 4 tablespoons rosemary
- ½ cup beef or chicken stock
- Salt and black pepper, to taste
- 1 tablespoon dried parsley
- 2 tablespoons onion powder
- 1 tablespoon garlic powder
- 1 tablespoon Italian seasoning
- 3 tablespoons olive oil

Directions

1. Mix onions, carrots, and potatoes in a large bowl. Sprinkle with two tablespoons of olive oil, add 2 tablespoons rosemary, season with salt and pepper. Stir to combine.
2. Transfer vegetable mixture to a slow cooker.
3. In another bowl combine parsley, onion and garlic powders, rosemary and Italian seasoning. Rub pork tenderloin with this mixture.

4. Heat 1 tablespoon of olive oil in a large skillet and brown pork from both sides for about 2-3 minutes.
5. Transfer browned meat on the top of the vegetables in a slow cooker.
6. Cover and cook on high for about 4 hours.
7. When ready, slice and serve with vegetables and juices.

Amazing Tender Chicken with Mushrooms

Prep time: 10 minutes, cook time: 6 hours, servings: 4-5

Ingredients

- 1 ½ pounds chicken breasts, skinless and trimmed of fat
- 2 cups chicken broth
- 1 middle onion, minced
- 6 cloves garlic, minced
- 1 tablespoon olive oil
- 1 tablespoon tomato paste
- 1 teaspoon dried thyme, crushed
- 1 lb fresh mushrooms, sliced
- 2 tablespoons white wine vinegar
- 2 tablespoons quick-cooking tapioca
- ½ cup Parmesan cheese
- 1 tablespoon dried parsley
- Salt and pepper for seasoning

Directions

1. In microwave-safe bowl mix onion, garlic, olive oil, tomato paste, thyme. Cook for about 5 minutes until onion becomes tender. Pour into a slow cooker.
2. Season chicken with salt and pepper.
3. In a bowl stir the chicken breasts, mushrooms, broth, vinegar and tapioca and put the mixture in the slow cooker.
4. Cover and cook on low for 4-6 hours.
5. Remove the chicken and shred it into large pieces using two forks.
6. Remove extra fat from the surface and place the chicken back into the slow cooker.
7. Add cheese and dried parsley.
8. Season to taste and serve with pasta or rice.

Spicy Pork Chili

Prep time: 10 minutes, cook time: 6 hours, servings: 6-8

Ingredients

- 2 pounds boneless pork, cut into 1/2-inch cubes
- 2 medium onions, chopped
- 3 garlic cloves, minced
- 1 can (15 oz) black beans, rinsed and drained
- 1 can (28 oz) crushed tomatoes
- 1 can (4 oz) chopped green chilies
- 2 cups corn, frozen
- 1 cup beef or chicken stock

- 1 tablespoon chili powder
- Salt and black pepper, to taste
- ¼ cup freshly chopped cilantro
- 1 tablespoon olive oil

Directions

1. Heat the olive oil in a skillet and cook pork over medium-high heat for 3-4 minutes from all sides until browned.
2. Transfer pork chunks with cooking juices to a slow cooker. Add tomatoes, onions, garlic, corn, stock, chilies and all seasoning.
3. Covet the lid and cook on low for 6 hours until meat is cooked and tender.
4. Sprinkle with freshly chopped cilantro and serve.

Zucchini and Tomato Spicy Pasta Sauce

Prep time: 7 minutes, cook time: 4 hours, servings: 4-6

Ingredients

- 2 cups zucchini, shredded
- 4 oz mushrooms, chopped
- ½ medium onion, chopped
- 4-5 medium tomatoes, diced
- 1 bay leaf
- ¼ cup fresh parsley, chopped
- 4 garlic cloves, minced
- ¼ teaspoon pepper
- 1 teaspoon garlic salt

- 1 teaspoon oregano
- 1 teaspoon basil
- 2 cans (8 oz) tomato sauce
- 2 tablespoon quick-cooking tapioca
- 1 pound turkey sausage (optional, you can cook both with or without meat)

Directions

1. Combine all vegetables in the large bowl.
2. Add spices, stir to combine.
3. Add everything in the slow cooker, cover and cook on low for 4 hours.
4. Stir and add sausages.
5. Season to taste and serve over pasta or spaghetti in your choice.

Delicious Chicken Penne

Prep time: 10 minutes, cook time: 3 ½ hours, servings: 4-5

Ingredients

- 1 pound chicken breasts, boneless
- 3 garlic cloves, minced
- 20 oz Marinara sauce
- 10 oz Alfredo sauce
- 10 oz Pesto sauce
- 10 oz Penne pasta, uncooked
- 2 tablespoons Italian seasoning
- ½ teaspoon salt

- ¼ teaspoon ground black pepper

Directions

1. Transfer chicken breasts to a slow cooker basket.
2. Combine three sauces and Italian seasoning in separate a bowl. Mix well.
3. Pour this mixture over the chicken. Cover and cook on low for 2 hours.
4. Uncover and add crushed garlic and uncooked pasta. Toss to combine.
5. Cover and cook for 1-2 hours more until penne is ready.
6. Remove chicken and cut into 1-inch pieces, then return to a slow cooker.
7. Serve hot. You may also sprinkle with shredded cheese if desired.

Adorable Crockpot Italian Chicken

Prep time: 10 minutes, cook time: 5 hours, servings: 4

Ingredients

- 2-4 chicken breasts, boneless and skinless
- 1 package (8 oz) cream cheese, softened
- 1 can cream of chicken soup
- 1 package Italian dressing seasoning
- Pasta or rice to serve

Directions

1. Prepare chicken and transfer in the slow cooker.

2. Combine softened cream cheese, cream of chicken and Italian seasoning and place evenly over the chicken.
3. Cover and cook on high up to 5 hours or until chicken will be prepared and fully tender.
4. Serve over cooked pasta or rice.

Shredded Lime Pork

Prep time: 15 minutes, cook time: 6 hours, servings: 6
Ingredients

- 3 pounds boneless pork shoulder butt roast
- 2 medium onions, chopped
- 2 garlic cloves, minced
- ½ cup water
- 2 chipotle peppers in adobo sauce, seeded and chopped
- 2 tablespoons molasses
- 2 cups broccoli florets
- 1 medium mango, peeled and chopped
- 2 tablespoons lime juice
- 2 teaspoons grated lime peel
- 1 tablespoon olive oil
- Salt and pepper, to taste

Directions

1. Cover the pork roast with salt and black pepper.

2. Preheat the olive oil in a skillet over high heat and brown meat from all sides for about 4-5 minutes. Replace meat to a slow cooker.
3. Using the same skillet with cooking juices sauté onion until tender, for 3-4 minutes. Add garlic and cook for 1 minute more.
4. Pour in ½ cup water, add chipotle peppers and molasses. Stir to combine. Pour this mixture over pork.
5. Cover and cook on high for 5 hours.
6. Remove the pork to a large plate and cool slightly. Shred meat with forks and return to a slow cooker.
7. Mix broccoli florets, mango, lime juice and lime peel in a bowl. Sprinkle with additional salt and pepper and stir in slow cooker. Bring to a boil and cook for 15-20 minutes, until veggies are cooked. Serve.

Jerky Chicken

Prep time: 10 minutes, cook time: 4 hours, servings: 6

Ingredients

- 6 large chicken legs
- 1 medium carrot, chopped
- 1 small onion, chopped
- 3 garlic cloves, crushed
- 2 teaspoons crushed red pepper
- 2 teaspoons garlic powder
- 2 teaspoons onion powder
- 2 teaspoons smoked paprika

- 2 teaspoons dried rosemary
- 1 teaspoon dried thyme
- 1 teaspoon ground ginger
- Salt and black pepper, to taste
- 1 teaspoon liquid smoke
- 3 tablespoons brown sugar
- 1 container of Caribbean jerk marinade
- 2 cups water

Directions

1. Place chicken legs in your slow cooker basket. Add all dried seasonings and ingredients.
2. Add carrots, onions, and garlic. Pour in marinade, liquid smoke and water to cover all the chicken.
3. Stir to combine well.
4. Cover and cook on high for 4 hours.
5. Serve and enjoy.

Slow Cooker Hawaiian Chicken with Pineapple

Prep time: 12 minutes, cook time: 4-6 hours, servings:6-8

Ingredients

- 5-6 chicken breasts, skinless and boneless
- ½ cup ketchup
- ½ teaspoon Worcestershire sauce
- 1 teaspoon mustard
- ½ pineapple with juice, crushed
- ½ cup brown sugar

- 1 can pineapple chunks

Directions

1. Prepare chicken breasts.
2. In large bowl mix ketchup, Worcestershire sauce, mustard, crushed pineapple with juice, brown sugar. Stir to combine.
3. Dip chicken breasts to the mixture and put them into the slow cooker.
4. Cover and cook on high for 4-6 hours or until chicken tender.
5. For the last 30 minutes of cooking time open the crockpot and dump in pineapple chunks.
6. Serve over rice or as you like.

Potato Stew with Vegetables and Spices

Prep time: 8 minutes, cook time: 5 hours, servings: 6-8

Ingredients

- 3 pounds potatoes, diced
- 1 medium onion, minced
- 4 medium tomatoes
- 2 teaspoon mustard seeds
- 1 teaspoon ground ginger
- 1 teaspoon garam masala
- 1 teaspoon turmeric
- ½ teaspoon ground cumin
- ½ teaspoon chili powder
- ¼ cup dried chili flakes

- 3 tablespoon Olive oil
- Salt and ground black pepper to taste

Directions

1. In a bowl mix spices expect of mustard seeds: ginger, garam masala, turmeric, cumin, chili powder.
2. Prepare vegetables, wash, peel and cube potatoes, mince onion.
3. Wash tomatoes, squeeze out seeds and chop them into little pieces.
4. Hit some olive oil, add mustard seeds and cook until popping.
5. Add onion; cook for near 5 minutes until transparent.
6. Add spices and cook for 3-4 minutes to get the flavor going.
7. Add cubed potatoes. Stir and make sure that every cube gets into spice mixture.
8. Add diced tomatoes.
9. Salt and add some ground pepper to taste.
10. Cook on low for 5 hours or until ready.

Buffalo Chicken Pasta

Prep time: 10 minutes, cook time: 4 hours, servings: 8-10

Ingredients

- 2 ½ pounds chicken breasts, boneless and skinless
- 1 large onion, chopped

- 3 garlic cloves, minced
- 1 pack (16 oz) penne pasta or spaghetti
- 2 cans (10 oz each) condensed cream of chicken soup
- 6 tablespoons Buffalo sauce
- 2 cups shredded Mozzarella cheese
- 1 ½ cups low-fat sour cream
- 5 tablespoons ranch dressing
- Salt and black pepper, to taste

Directions

1. Cut the chicken tenders into 1-inch cubes and place to a slow cooker. Add onions, garlic, condensed cream, sauce, salt and pepper. Stir to combine.
2. Cover and cook for 4 hours.
3. Meanwhile, cook pasta according to package directions for almost cooked. Drain.
4. When chicken cooked, add cheese and stir until melted. Add pasta, sour cream and ranch dressing.

Stuffed Peppers

Prep time: 20 minutes, cook time: 3 hours, servings: 7

Ingredients

- 7 medium-sized any color peppers, cored
- ½ cup frozen corn, defrosted
- 1 medium onion, chopped
- 1 pound ground beef, browned
- ½ can (16 oz) tomato sauce

- 1 cup Cheddar cheese, shredded
- 2 garlic cloves, minced
- 4 tablespoons water
- 1 teaspoon salt or less
- 1/3 teaspoon black pepper

Directions

1. Mix all ingredients together, except cheese. Stir to combine well.
2. Remove tops of peppers and core them. Stuff peppers with meat mixture.
3. Top each pepper with shredded cheese and transfer to a slow cooker basket.
4. Pour in 4 tablespoons of water, cover and cook on high for 3-4 hours, until meat becomes ready.
5. Serve.

Bacon Cheese Potatoes

Prep time: 5 minutes, cook time: 8 hours, servings: 4

Ingredients

- ¼ pound bacon, diced
- 2-3 medium onion, sliced
- 5 medium potatoes, sliced
- ½ pound cheddar cheese, sliced
- 1 tablespoon butter
- Salt and ground pepper for seasoning
- Green onion (optional)

Directions

1. Put foil on the bottom of the slow cooker, leaving enough to cover the potatoes.
2. Make a layer half of potatoes, bacon, onion and cheese. Season with salt and pepper to taste and dot with butter.
3. Do the same layers with the rest of ingredients. Season to taste and dot with butter.
4. Cover everything with remaining foil.
5. Cover and cook on low for 8-10 hours.

Pork Chops with Tomatoes

Prep time: 15 minutes, cook time: 8 hours, servings: 6-8

Ingredients

- 6-8 pork chops, bone-in
- 1 large onion, chopped
- 2 medium carrots, chopped
- 1 can (15 oz) diced tomatoes
- 1 teaspoon dried oregano
- 2 teaspoon dried dill
- 3 tablespoons balsamic vinegar
- 1 tablespoon olive oil
- 1 teaspoon salt
- ¼ teaspoon black pepper

Directions

1. Heat the olive oil in a large skillet. Brown pork chops in batches for 4-5 minutes until brown and then transfer to a slow cooker.
2. In the same skillet sauté onions and carrots for 3-4 minutes and also transfer to a slow cooker.
3. Add dry herbs, stir in tomatoes and vinegar. Cover and cook on low for 8 hours.
4. Serve.

Herbs & Wine Veal

Prep time: 10 minutes, cook time: 6-7 hours, servings: 4-5

Ingredients

- 2 pounds veal cut
- 4-5 garlic cloves
- 1 teaspoon dried thyme
- 1 teaspoon dried rosemary
- 1 teaspoon dried sage
- ½ cup butter
- 1 bottle dry red wine
- Salt and black pepper, to taste

Directions

1. Mix all dry ingredients and herbs in a bowl. Rub the meat with herbs and transfer to a slow cooker basket.
2. Pour in wine to cover the meat. If it's not enough you may pour in some water.

3. Lay butter on top of the meat.
4. Cover and cook on low for 6-7 hours until meat tender.
5. Serve with mashed potatoes, noodles or rice.

Tender Pork Chops

Prep time: 6 minutes, cook time: 4 hours, servings: 4

Ingredients

- 4 pork loin chops (4 oz in each), boneless
- 1 can (14 oz) chicken broth
- ¾ cup all-purpose flour, divided
- ½ teaspoon ground mustard
- ½ teaspoon garlic pepper blend
- 2 tablespoon canola oil
- Salt for seasoning

Directions

1. Take 1 large plastic bag. Put in it ½ cup flour, mustard, garlic pepper, salt.
2. Add pork chops, one at a time. Shake well to be sure that meat covers evenly.
3. Brown pork in a large skillet in oil on both sides.
4. Put browned pork chops to the slow cooker.
5. Place remaining flour in a bowl, add chicken broth. Whisk until smooth.
6. Pour this mixture over chops.
7. Cover and cook on low for 3-4 hours or until meat is tender.

8. Serve until warm and enjoy.

Delicious Meatballs with Currant Jelly

Prep time: 5 minutes, cook time: 4 hours, servings: 6

Ingredients

- 2 pounds frozen (pre-cooked) meatballs
- 1 cup of red currant jelly
- 1 jar (8 ounces) chili sauce
- 2 tablespoons olive oil
- Salt and black pepper, to taste

Directions

1. Add frozen meatballs to a slow cooker and sprinkle them with olive oil. Stir to combine to coat the meatball thoroughly.
2. Cook on high for 3 hours.
3. Meanwhile, combine currant jelly and chili sauce in a medium-sized bowl. Pour the mixture in a slow cooker and cook for another hour.
4. Serve and enjoy!

Pork Chops Barbecue with Apples and Onions

Prep time: 5 minutes, cook time: 4 hours, servings: 5

Ingredients

- 4 large apples, cored and sliced
- 2 large onions, sliced
- 8 large pork chops
- ½ cup water
- 1 jar (8 oz) barbecue sauce
- 1 teaspoon salt
- 1/4 teaspoon black pepper

Directions

1. Cover pork chops with salt and pepper and transfer to a slow cooker.
2. Slice apples and onions and cover the meat. Pour in water, close the lid and cook on high for 3 hours.
3. Meanwhile, combine barbecue sauce with water.
4. When meat is almost ready, open the lid and stir in sauce to a slow cooker. Cook for 30-40 minutes more.
5. Serve hot and enjoy.

Hoisin Pork Wraps

Prep time: 23 minutes, cook time: 7 hours, servings: 8

Ingredients

- 2 pounds pork loin boneless
- ½ cup hoisin sauce
- 1 cup water
- 2 teaspoon fresh ginger, grated
- 2 medium carrots, sliced
- 2 tablespoons green onions, thinly sliced
- 1 tablespoon vinegar
- 3 cups red cabbage, shredded
- Salt and black pepper, to taste

Directions

1. In the large bowl Combine shredded cabbage, carrots, green onions, sugar, and vinegar. Mix well and set aside.
2. In another bowl combine hoisin sauce and grated ginger. Add salt and pepper and rub the mixture all over pork. Transfer to a slow cooker pot, pour in water, and cook for 7 hours until ready.
3. Shred the pork loin with two forks and return to a slow cooker. Cook uncovered for 10 minutes and serve with vegetable mixture.

Black Beans and Beef Stew

Prep time: 5 minutes, cook time: 8 hours, servings: 4

Ingredients

- 1 pound beef
- 1 large onion, chopped
- 1 large potato, diced

- 1 large carrot, chopped
- 2 cans (15 oz each) black beans, rinsed and drained
- 4 cups chicken broth
- 1 teaspoon chili powder
- 1 teaspoon ground cumin
- ½ teaspoon salt
- ¼ teaspoon ground black pepper
- 1 tablespoon olive oil

Directions

1. Cut beef into 1-inch pieces and transfer to a slow cooker pot. Add all another ingredients, and season with salt, pepper, cumin, and chili powder. Pour in broth and stir to combine well.
2. Close the lid and cook for 7-8 hours on low.
3. Serve with freshly chopped herbs on your preference.

Asian Pork Chops

Prep time: 20 minutes, cook time: 6 hours, servings: 4

Ingredients

- 8 pork chops, boneless
- 3 tablespoons sugar
- 4 garlic cloves, chopped
- 1 teaspoon grated ginger
- ½ cup soy sauce
- ½ cup ketchup
- Salt and ground black pepper, to taste

Directions

1. In a large mixing bowl combine pork chops, sugar, grated ginger, soy sauce, ketchup, and season with salt and pepper.
2. Transfer marinated pork chops to a slow cooker pot and cook on high for 6 hours.
3. Serve with steamed vegetables or egg noodles.

Apple Cider Beef Roast with Ginger

Prep time: 15 minutes, cook time: 7 hours, servings: 6-8

Ingredients

- 3 pounds beef pot roast
- 2 medium-sized onions, chopped
- 4 garlic cloves, minced
- 2 teaspoons grated ginger
- 1 teaspoon grated cinnamon
- 1 teaspoon salt
- 2 cups apple cider

Directions

1. Place beef into a large bowl. Add chopped onions and minced garlic. Add ginger, cinnamon, salt, and pour in apple cider. Refrigerate for at least 1 hour.
2. Transfer the meat with all juices to a slow cooker pan. Secure the lid and cook for 7 hours on low, until meat becomes tender.
3. Slice beef and serve.

Cabbage and Kielbasa

Prep time: 5 minutes, cook time: 7 hours, servings: 6

Ingredients

- 1 small cabbage head (about 2 pounds), cut into large wedges
- 2 medium-sized onions, sliced
- 1 cup chicken or vegetable stock
- 1 tablespoon mustard
- 1 pound kielbasa, cut into 1-inch pieces
- 1 teaspoon salt
- Grated black pepper, to taste
- 1 tablespoon olive oil

Directions

1. Place cabbage wedges to a slow cooker. Add sliced onions, mustard and chicken stock. Season with salt and pepper and stir to combine.
2. Scatter chopped kielbasa over the cabbage.
3. Cover and cook on low for 6-7 hours.
4. Serve and enjoy.

Clean Eating Crock Pot Chuck Roast

Prep time: 45 minutes, cook time: 5 hours, servings: 8

Ingredients

- 3 pounds chuck roast
- 4 large potatoes
- 1 large carrot, chopped
- 2 medium onions, diced
- 3 garlic cloves, minced
- 2 cups water
- 1 cup chicken or beef stock
- 1 teaspoon Italian seasoning
- 1 teaspoon salt
- ¼ teaspoon black pepper, ground

Directions

1. Cut vegetables and transfer to a slow cooker.
2. Rub chuck roast with salt, pepper, and Italian seasoning and place over diced vegetables. Pour in stock and water. Make sure that liquid is covering all ingredients.
3. Close the lid and cook on high for 5 hours.
4. Serve with juices and enjoy.

Roast Pork Loin

Prep time: 20 minutes, cook time: 5 hours, servings: 8

Ingredients

- 3 pound pork loin, boneless
- 3 cloves garlic, minced
- 2 cups chicken or vegetable stock
- 1 teaspoon Worcestershire sauce
- 2 teaspoons smoked paprika
- 1 tablespoon fresh thyme, chopped
- 2 tablespoons lemon juice
- ½ teaspoon fresh ground black pepper
- 1 teaspoon salt
- 2 tablespoons olive oil

Directions

1. In a small bowl combine minced garlic, fresh thyme, smoked paprika, black pepper, and salt. Rub the meat with this herb mixture.
2. Heat the olive oil in a skillet over high heat and brown pork loin from both sides for about 5 minutes. Transfer meat to a slow cooker.
3. Pour in stock, close the lid and cook on high for 5 hours.
4. Slice pork loin and serve hot.

Slow Cooker Beef Brisket

Prep time: 20 minutes, cook time: 6 hours, servings: 8

Ingredients

- 2 pounds beef brisket without fat
- 4 tablespoons ketchup
- 1 cup water
- 1 large onion, chopped
- 2 tablespoons vinegar
- 1 tablespoon mustard
- 1 tablespoon sugar
- ½ teaspoon salt
- ¼ teaspoon black pepper

Directions

1. Cover beef brisket with salt and pepper and transfer to a slow cooker. Add chopped onion and pour in water.
2. Close the lid and cook on low for 6 hours.
3. Meanwhile, combine ketchup, vinegar, mustard and couple tablespoons of water in the mixing bowl. Sauté the mixture in a heatproof pan over low heat for 10-15 minutes.
4. When meat becomes ready, slice it and cover with sauce. Enjoy.

Smoked Up Baby Potatoes with Beef

Prep time: 10 minutes, cook time: 5 hours, servings: 6

Ingredients

- 2 pounds beef
- 2 pounds baby potatoes
- 2 large tomatoes, chopped
- 3 garlic cloves, minced
- 1 medium-sized onion, chopped
- 1 tablespoon smoked paprika
- ½ teaspoon chili powder
- 3 tablespoons ketchup
- 1 teaspoon cumin
- 5 tablespoons barbecue sauce
- ¼ cup salsa
- 1 cup frozen corn
- 1 tablespoon olive oil
- Salt and pepper, to taste

Directions

1. Cut beef into 1-inch cubes and transfer to a slow cooker. Add 1 tablespoon of olive oil and brown meat using Sauté mode.
2. Add baby potatoes, onions, tomatoes, and garlic, chili powder, cumin, salsa and barbecue sauces. Mix well and cook on high for 4-5 hours until meat is almost done.

3. Add frozen corn, season with salt and pepper and cook for 1 hour more.
4. Serve and enjoy.

Italian Chicken with Peppers & Spaghetti

Prep time: 15 minutes, cook time: 3 ½ hours, servings: 5-6

Ingredients

- 5-6 chicken breast halves, boneless skinless
- 1 jar (24 oz) spaghetti sauce
- Hot cooked pasta
- 1 large onion, sliced
- 2 garlic cloves, minced
- 1 each small green, sweet yellow and red peppers
- ¼ cup grated Parmesan cheese
- 1 teaspoon dried oregano
- 1 teaspoon dried basil
- Salt and black pepper, to taste

Directions

1. Place chicken breasts in the crock pot. Add onions and garlic, chopped peppers, and dried herbs. Season with salt and pepper, to taste.
2. Cover and cook on high for 3-4 hours until chicken tender.
3. Serve with cooked spaghetti and top with shredded Parmesan cheese.

Delicious Chicken Cordon Bleu

Prep time: 10 minutes, cook time: 6 hours, servings: 6-8

Ingredients

- 6 chicken breast halves, boneless and skinless
- 10 oz condensed cream of chicken soup
- 1 cup milk
- 4 oz ham, sliced
- 4 oz Swiss cheese, sliced
- 8 oz herbed dry breadcrumbs
- ¼ cut butter, melted

Directions

1. In a small bowl combine condensed cream of chicken soup and milk.
2. Pour enough soup into the slow cooker to cover the bottom.
3. Lay chicken breasts over the sauce.
4. Cover with ham and Swiss cheese slices.
5. Pour the remaining soup mixture over the layers, trying to distribute between layers.
6. Sprinkle herbed breadcrumbs on top, drizzle with butter over breadcrumbs.
7. Cover with lid and cook on low for 5-6 hours.

Beer Chili Beans with Bratwurst Sausage

Prep time: 10 minutes, cook time: 5 hours, servings: 6-8

Ingredients

- 1 pound fully cooked beer bratwurst links, sliced
- 1 large onion, chopped
- 2 garlic cloves, crushed
- 2 tablespoons chili seasoning
- 1 can (15 oz) Southwestern black beans, undrained
- 1 can (15 oz) pinto beans, rinsed and drained
- 1 can (15 oz) white kidney or cannellini beans, rinsed and drained
- 1 can (10 oz) diced tomatoes and green chilies, undrained
- 1 can (14 oz) Italian diced tomatoes, undrained
- ½ teaspoon salt
- Chopped fresh parsley, optional

Directions

1. Cut beer bratwurst sausage into 1-inch slices and place to a slow cooker. Add onions and garlic, and pour in beans and tomatoes. Season with salt and chili mix. Stir to combine.
2. Cover and cook on low for 4,5-5 hours. When ready sprinkle with freshly chopped parsley and serve warm.

Salsa Verde Pork

Prep time: 8 minutes, cook time: 7-8 hours, servings: 4

Ingredients

- 2 pounds pork sirloin or loin
- 1 jar (16 oz) Salsa Verde

- 1 can (4 oz) green chilies, diced
- 1 tablespoon ground cumin
- 1 teaspoon salt for seasoning

Directions

1. Spray slow cooker with cooking spray.
2. Freely sprinkle salt over pork. Place meat to the cooker.
3. Pour a jar of Salsa Verde over pork. Then add diced green chilies and sprinkle with ground cumin.
4. Cover the crock pot and cook on low for at least 8 hours.
5. Shred pork and put back to the sauce.
6. You may serve with any topping you like: cheese, sour cream, tomatoes, etc.
7. Enjoy!

Tender Beef Stroganoff

Prep time: 6 minutes, cook time: 5-6 hours, servings: 4-5

Ingredients

- 2 pounds stew beef
- ½ cup beef broth
- 16 oz fresh mushrooms, sliced
- 2 packages onion soup mix
- 3 tablespoon Worcestershire sauce
- 2 ½ cup sour cream
- 4 oz cream cheese, softened

- 1 package cooked egg noodles for serving

Directions

1. Put stew meat, broth, sliced mushrooms, soup mix, Worcestershire sauce into the slow cooker and cook on low for 4-6 hours until meat prepared.'
2. After that add sour cream and cream cheese into the cooker, stir the mixture until combined and smooth.
3. Serve over cooked egg noodles.
4. Enjoy.

Stewed Slow Cooker Round Steak

Prep time: 15 minutes, cook time: 7 hours, servings: 5-6

Ingredients

- 2 pounds beef steak, cut into 1-inch strips
- 2 medium onions, sliced
- 1 cup fresh mushrooms, sliced
- 2 bell peppers, cored and sliced
- 1 can (15 oz) diced tomatoes with juices
- 4 tablespoons soy sauce
- ½ tablespoon dried oregano
- ½ tablespoon dried dill
- 1 teaspoon salt
- ¼ teaspoon black pepper

Directions

1. Cut the meat and place to a large bowl. Sprinkle with salt and pepper and stir to combine. Make sure that all sides of the meat are covered with seasoning.
2. Transfer marinated meat to a slow cooker.
3. Add sliced onions and mushrooms, stir in diced tomatoes and soy sauce. Stir to combine.
4. Cover and cook on low for 6-7 hours.
5. Serve with mashed potatoes or egg noodles.

Sweet Potatoes with Coconut and Pecans

Prep time: 10 minutes, cook time: 4 hours, servings: 8

Ingredients

- 3 pounds sweet potatoes, cubed into 1-inch pieces
- ½ cup pecans, chopped
- ½ cup coconut flakes
- 4 tablespoons sugar
- ½ teaspoon ground cinnamon
- ½ teaspoon coconut extract
- ½ teaspoon vanilla extract
- 2 tablespoons butter, melted
- A pinch of salt

Directions

1. Mix chopped pecans, coconut flakes, sugar, cinnamon and salt in a bowl. Add melted butter and stir to combine.

2. Place sweet potatoes to a slow cooker and cover with pecan mixture.
3. Cook on low for 4 hours until potatoes become tender and cooked.
4. Add coconut and vanilla extracts, stir to combine and serve.

Mom's Amazing Pot Roast

Prep time: 12 minutes, cook time: 4 hours, servings: 3-4

Ingredients

- 1 pound pot roast
- 3 cubes beef bouillon
- 10 oz beef broth
- 3 garlic cloves, minced
- ¼ teaspoon, Cayenne pepper
- 2 tablespoon cumin
- 1 teaspoon oregano
- ¼ teaspoon ground pepper
- 2 middle carrots, grated

Directions

1. Cut meat into 2-3 inch cubes and place into the slow cooker.
2. Combine beef broth, bouillon cubes, garlic, cayenne pepper, cumin, oregano and ground pepper.
3. Pour this mixture over the meat in the slow cooker.

4. Cover and cook on high for 3-4 hours or until meat ready and tender.
5. Serve with rice or potatoes.

Easy Beef Steak

Prep time: 10 minutes, cook time: 6 hours, servings: 4-5

Ingredients

- 2 pounds beef round steak
- 1 large onion, sliced
- 1 garlic clove, minced
- 2 tablespoons all-purpose flour
- ½ cup tomato paste
- ½ teaspoon salt
- ¼ teaspoon ground black pepper

Directions

1. Divide steak into 4 pieces. Cover each piece with flour, salt and pepper.
2. Slice onion and transfer to a slow cooker.
3. Lay the meat over onions and cover with tomato paste. Cover and cook on low for 5-6 hours until meat is tender.
4. Serve with cooked rice or potatoes.

Effortless Side Dishes

Spicy Quinoa Bowl

Prep time: 7 minutes, cook time: 7-8 hours, servings: 5-7

Ingredients

- 1 cup dried quinoa, rinsed
- 1 can (15 oz) black beans, rinsed and drained
- 1 can (15 oz) fire roasted diced tomatoes
- 1 medium-sized zucchini, diced
- 4-5 small red peppers, diced
- 3 garlic cloves, minced
- 2 cups water
- 1/2 cup frozen corn
- 1 package taco seasoning
- Salt and black pepper, to taste
- Freshly chopped cilantro and parsley for garnish (optional)
- Shredded Parmesan cheese for garnish (optional)

Directions

1. Place quinoa, beans, tomatoes, minced garlic, diced zucchini, and red peppers to a slow cooker basket. Season with salt and pepper, and pour in enough water to cover the mixture.
2. Cover and cook on low for 6 - 1/2 hours.
3. Open and add corn. Cook on high for 30-40 minutes more.
4. Serve and top with chopped herbs and cheese.

Jamaican Curry Chicken

Prep time: 15 minutes, cook time: 2 hours, servings: 5-6

Ingredients

- 2 pounds chicken breasts, skinless and boneless
- 2 medium-sized onions, chopped
- 2 large potatoes, peeled and diced
- 2 garlic cloves
- ½ bell pepper, diced
- 2 tablespoons Jamaican spices
- 3 tablespoons Curry powder
- ½ tablespoon dried thyme
- 1 cup water
- ¼ teaspoon black pepper
- 1 teaspoon salt

Directions

1. Wash chicken, dry with kitchen towels, and cut into 2-inch pieces. Transfer to a large bowl.
2. Add diced potatoes, onions, garlic, bell peppers and all seasoning. Stir to combine well and set aside at least for 30 minutes.
3. Place chicken & vegetable mixture to a slow cooker and pour in water.
4. Cover and cook on high for 2 hours.
5. Serve hot. Sprinkle with freshly chopped herbs if desired.

Meaty Tomato Sauce

Prep time: 10 minutes, cook time: 4 hours, servings: 5-6

Ingredients

- 2 pounds ground beef
- 1 large onion, chopped
- 3 garlic cloves, crushed
- 1 can (15 oz) tomatoes
- 4 tablespoons tomato paste
- 1 tablespoon dried oregano
- 1 tablespoon dried basil
- ½ cup water
- 1 teaspoon salt
- ¼ teaspoon black pepper
- 1 tablespoon olive oil

Directions

1. Heat olive oil in a large skillet over medium-high heat. Sauté onions and garlic until golden for 4-5 minutes. Add ground beef and brown meat until no longer pink.
2. Transfer to a slow cooker.
3. Add dried herbs, tomatoes and tomato paste, pour in water and stir to combine. Season with salt and pepper, cover and cook on high for 4 hours.
4. Serve with noodles or steamed rice.

Delicious Chicken with Mushrooms

Prep time: 17 minutes, cook time: 3-4 hours, servings: 5-7

Ingredients

- 2 ½ pounds chicken breast, without bones and skin
- 1 medium onion, chopped
- 2-3 garlic cloves, minced
- 3 cups fresh mushrooms on your preference, sliced
- 1 cup chicken or vegetable stock
- 3 tablespoons tomato paste
- 1/2 cup dry red wine
- 1 tablespoon dried basil
- 1 tablespoon dried oregano
- 1 teaspoon salt
- ¼ teaspoon black pepper
- ¼ cup Parmesan cheese, grated

Directions

1. Lay sliced mushrooms, onions, and garlic on the bottom of your slow cooker.
2. Cut chicken into 2-inch pieces and place on top of the vegetables.
3. In a separate bowl combine stock, tomato paste, wine, basil, oregano, salt, and pepper. Mix well.
4. Pour the mixture over chicken and vegetables.
5. Cover and cook on high for 3-4 hours, until chicken is tender.

6. Serve with noodles or mashed potatoes and top with grated Parmesan cheese.

Beef and Broccoli Penne

Prep time: 10 minutes, cook time: 2-3 hours, servings: 5

Ingredients

- 1 pound ground beef
- 1 broccoli head (nearly 1 pound) cut into florets
- 1 large onion, sliced
- 2 garlic cloves, minced
- 1 teaspoon dried oregano
- 1 teaspoon dried basil
- 1 teaspoon dried thyme
- 1 can (14 oz) diced tomatoes with juices
- 2 cups beef or chicken stock
- 2 tablespoons tomato paste
- 2 cups Penne, cooked
- ½ cup shredded Cheddar cheese
- 1 tablespoon olive oil
- Salt and pepper, to taste

Directions

1. Heat the olive oil in a large skillet over medium heat and cook ground beef with garlic until no longer pink, breaking meat apart with wooden spoon.
2. Transfer browned meat to a slow cooker.

3. Add broccoli florets, onions, tomatoes with juices, and tomato paste to a slow cooker. Season with salt and pepper, add dried herbs and pour in stock.
4. Cover and cook on high for 2-3 hours.
5. Serve with cooker Penne pasta and top with shredded cheese.

Pesto Chicken with Sun Dried Tomatoes

Prep time: 5 minutes, cook time: 3-4 hours, servings: 6-8

Ingredients

- 6-8 chicken thighs
- 1 package Italian seasoning mix
- ½ cup basil pesto
- ½ cup sun dried tomatoes, chopped
- 1/3 cup half & half
- 1/3 cup chicken or vegetable stock
- 3 teaspoons butter
- 1 teaspoon olive oil
- 1 teaspoon salt
- ¼ teaspoon ground black pepper

Directions

1. Heat the olive oil and butter in a skillet over high heat. Brown chicken thighs on both sides for about 4-5 minutes.
2. Transfer chicken to a slow cooker.

3. Pour in stock and season with Italian seasoning. Stir in pesto and tomatoes. Add salt and pepper, stir to combine well.
4. Cover and cook on high for 3-4 hours.
5. When cooked, stir in half & half.
6. Serve with cooked pasta, mashed potatoes or vegetables.

Amazing Almond Chicken with Curry

Prep time: 10 minutes, cook time: 6 hours, servings: 6

Ingredients

- 8 medium chicken thighs with skin
- ½ cup chicken stock
- 2 garlic cloves, minced
- 1 tablespoon curry powder
- 1 cup almond milk
- 1 cup chopped leeks
- 1 cup almonds, roasted and chopped
- 1 teaspoon salt
- 1 tablespoon of olive oil

Directions

1. In the large skillet preheat olive oil over medium heat and sauté leeks for 3-4 minutes, until tender. Add garlic and cook for 3 minutes more, stirring occasionally. Transfer to a slow cooker.
2. Add chicken thighs, curry powder, almond milk, and season with salt.

3. Close the lid and cook on high for 5-6 hours.
4. When ready, stir in almonds and serve hot. Enjoy!

Salsa Chicken in Sour Cream

Prep time: 10 minutes, cook time: 3 hours, servings: 5

Ingredients
- 3 pounds chicken breasts, boneless and skinless, cut in halves
- 6-8 slices cooked ham
- 3 tablespoons taco seasoning
- 2 cups salsa
- 1/2 cup low-fat sour cream

Directions

1. Cut chicken in halves and cover each piece with ham. Roll up and secure with toothpicks. Rub with taco seasoning.
2. Transfer chicken pieces to a slow cooker and pour over with salsa and sour cream.
3. Cover the lid and cook on high for 3 hours, until chicken becomes ready.
4. Serve with mashed potatoes or steamed rice.

Orange Chicken

Prep time: 5 minutes, cook time: 6 hours, servings: 4

Ingredients

- 2 pounds chicken breasts, skinless and boneless, cut into 1-inch pieces
- ½ cup all-purpose flour
- ½ cup hoisin sauce
- ½ cup orange marmalade
- 4 tablespoons soy sauce
- 1 teaspoon grated ginger
- ¼ teaspoon ground black pepper
- ½ teaspoon salt
- 1 tablespoon olive oil

Directions

1. Cut chicken breasts and lightly coat with flour. Sprinkle slow cooker pot with olive oil and brown chicken pieces using Sauté mode. Cook for 5-7 minutes. When lightly brown, season chicken with ginger, salt, and pepper. Add hoisin sauce, marmalade, soy sauce and stir to combine.
2. Cover the lid and cook on low for 5-6 hours, until tender.
3. Serve with grilled vegetables or mashed potatoes.

Creole Chicken Stew

Prep time: 10 minutes, cook time: 4 hours, servings: 5-6

Ingredients

- 2 pounds chicken breasts
- 2 medium onions, sliced
- 4 stalks celery, chopped
- 3 large tomatoes, chopped
- 1 large green bell pepper, chopped
- 4 garlic cloves, minced
- 3 tablespoons tomato paste
- 1 cup chicken stock
- ¼ teaspoon black pepper
- ½ teaspoon salt
- 1 tablespoon Cajun seasoning
- 1 teaspoon dried thyme
- 2 tablespoons olive oil
- Freshly chopped parsley for garnish

Directions

1. Sprinkle slow cooker pot with the olive oil and set the cooker on Sauté mode. Add sliced onions and minced garlic and sauté for 5-7 minutes, until tender. Add celery and bell pepper, stir to combine and cook for another 3-5 minutes.

2. Add diced tomatoes, tomato paste and pour in stock. Mix well and sauté for 2-3 minutes more.
3. Cut chicken breasts into 2-inch pieces and transfer to a slow cooker. Season with salt, pepper, thyme and Cajun mixture. Close the lid and cook on high for 3 hours.
4. Garnish with freshly chopped parsley, serve and enjoy.

Creamy Chicken with Noodles

Prep time: 7 minutes, cook time: 2 hours, servings: 5-6
Ingredients

- 2 pounds cooked chicken breasts, cut into large chunks
- 1 medium onion, chopped
- 1 little carrot, diced
- 12 oz condensed cream of chicken soup
- 6 tablespoons mayonnaise
- 2 tablespoons all-purpose flour
- 1 cup frozen broccoli florets, defrosted
- 1 teaspoon curry powder
- Salt and black pepper, to taste
- 2 cups cooked egg noodles

Directions

1. In a large bowl combine cooked chicken breasts, chopped onions, carrots, condensed cream,

mayonnaise, flour, defrosted broccoli florets. Add curry powder, salt and pepper, to taste. Mix well.
2. Transfer the mixture to a slow cooker basket, cover the lid and cook on high for 2 hours.
3. When ready, serve the chicken with egg noodles.
4. You can also sprinkle with grated cheese to your taste.

White Chicken Chili

Prep time: 30 minutes, cook time: 6 hours, servings: 6

Ingredients

- 2 pounds chicken breasts, skinless and boneless
- 3 cans (15 ounces each) northern beans
- 2 cans (8 ounces each) green chilies, chopped
- 2 cups chicken or vegetable stock
- 1 cup water
- 1 large onion, chopped
- 2 garlic cloves, minced
- 2 teaspoons of cumin
- 6 tablespoons fresh cilantro, chopped
- 1 teaspoon chili powder
- 1 teaspoon salt

Directions

1. Cut chicken breasts into 1-inch cubes and transfer to a slow cooker. Add chilies, beans, onions, cumin, and garlic. Season with salt and pepper and pour in water and chicken stock.

2. Close the lid and cook on low for nearly 6 hours until chicken becomes ready.
3. When ready, stir in chopped cilantro and cook uncovered for another 10-20 minutes.
4. Serve.

Delicious Chicken with Noodles

Prep time: 10 minutes, cook time: 3 hours, servings: 4

Ingredients

- 1 pound chicken breasts, skinless and boneless
- 2 pack uncooked egg noodles
- 4 cups water
- 2 cups chicken or vegetable stock
- 1 large onion, chopped
- 2 medium-sized carrots, grated
- 1 teaspoon dried basil
- ½ teaspoon salt
- ¼ teaspoon ground black pepper

Directions

1. Wash up chicken breasts and transfer to a slow cooker pot. Add onions and carrots, season with salt, pepper and basil. Pour in water and stock and stir to combine.
2. Close the lid and cook on low for 4 hours.

3. Open your crock pot and cut chicken breast into 1-2 inch pieces. Transfer chicken cubes in the slow cooker and add noodles. Cook for another 15-20 minutes.
4. Serve and enjoy.

Chicken Paprikash Noodles

Prep time: 8 minutes, cook time: 5 hours, servings: 8

Ingredients

- 2 pounds chicken breasts, boneless and skinless
- 2 medium onions, diced
- 3 garlic cloves, minced
- 2 cups egg noodles, cooked
- Couple bay leaves
- ¼ teaspoon ground black pepper
- 1 teaspoon paprika
- ½ cup chicken stock
- 1 cup cream cheese
- 1 teaspoon salt
- 2 tablespoons olive oil

Directions

1. Sprinkle slow cooker pot with olive oil and sauté garlic and onion for about 5-7 minutes, stirring occasionally.

2. Cut chicken breasts and place to a slow cooker. Sauté for 5 minutes more. Add bay leaves, black pepper, salt, paprika. Pour in chicken stock and mix well. Cover the lid and cook for 5 hours, until cooked.
3. Serve with cooked egg noodles and stir in cream cheese. Enjoy.

Amazing Chicken Fajitas Ala Pot

Prep time: 20 minutes, cook time: 5 hours, servings: 4

Ingredients

- 4 large chicken breasts, skinless and boneless
- Juice of 1 whole lime (medium-sized)
- 1 medium-sized yellow onion, chopped
- 1 small bell pepper, cut
- ½ cup green chilies, diced
- ½ teaspoon smoked paprika
- 1 teaspoon cumin
- 1 cup Salsa
- 2 tablespoon olive oil
- 1 teaspoon sea salt

Directions

1. Cut breast into 1-inch pieces and transfer to a slow cooker. Sprinkle them with smoked paprika, cumin, and chili powder, salt and lemon juice.
2. Stir in Salsa and diced chilies.
3. Meanwhile, preheat olive oil in the large skillet over medium heat and sauté onions and garlic for 5 minutes. Transfer to a slow cooker and stir to combine.
4. Close the lid and cook on low for 5 hours.
5. Serve with cooked rice or mashed potatoes and enjoy!

Turkey with Onion-Garlic Sauce

Prep time: 10 minutes, cook time: 5 hours, servings: 8

Ingredients

- 4 large sized skinless turkey thighs
- 4 medium-sized onions, sliced
- 6 garlic cloves, chopped
- ¼ cup dry white wine
- ¼ teaspoon cayenne pepper
- ½ teaspoon salt

Directions

1. Lay sliced onions and chopped garlic on the bottom of your slow cooker pot. Season with salt and cayenne pepper and pour in white wine.
2. Transfer turkey thighs over wine mixture and close the lid.
3. Cook on high for 5 hours.
4. Remove the turkey and shred it using forks. Discard bones and return meat to a slow cooker.
5. Stir to combine and serve hot.

Amazing Soup Recipes

Chicken Soup with Spinach and Herbs

Prep time: 10 minutes, cook time: 4-5 hours, servings: 4-5

Ingredients

- 1 pound chicken things, boneless and skinless, cut into ½ inch pieces
- 1 can (16 oz) kidney beans, rinsed and well drained
- 14 oz chicken broth
- 1 onion, chopped
- 1 sweet red pepper, chopped
- 2 tablespoons tomato paste
- 3 garlic cloves, minced
- ½ teaspoon fresh rosemary, minced
- ½ teaspoon fresh thyme, minced
- ½ teaspoon dried oregano, crushed
- ¼ teaspoon salt
- ¼ teaspoon pepper
- 3 cups fresh baby spinach
- ¼ cup Parmesan cheese, shredded

Directions

1. Prepare all ingredients.
2. Combine them in the slow cooker, cover and cook on low for 4-5 hours or until chicken is tender.
3. Stir in baby spinach.
4. Cover and cook for 30 minutes until spinach is wilted.

5. Top with cheese.

Easy Potato Soup

Prep time: 25 minutes, cook time: 5 hours, servings: 5-6

Ingredients

- 2 pounds potatoes, cubed and divided
- 2 cups water
- 3 tablespoon butter
- 2/3 cup sour cream
- 1/2 cup Cheddar cheese, shredded
- 1/2 pound cooked ham, cubed
- 2 celery ribs, chopped
- 1 medium onion, chopped
- 2 garlic cloves, minced
- 1 teaspoon paprika
- Salt and black pepper, to taste

Directions

1. Add 1 ½ pound of cubed potatoes in a saucepan and bring to a boil over high heat. Reduce heat and cook for 12 minutes or until cooked.
2. Remove from the heat and mash potatoes with potato masher. Stir in butter.
3. In a slow cooker add cooked ham, chopped celery, onions, and garlic. Season with salt, pepper and paprika, and stir it remaining potatoes. Also add

mashed potatoes and shredded cheese. Stir to combine.
4. Cover with lid and cook on low for 4,5-5 hours, until potatoes are tender. Add sour cream and serve.

Simple Pea Soup

Prep time: 5 minutes, cook time: 4 hours, servings: 7-8

Ingredients

- 1 pack (16 oz) dried split peas
- ½ pound cooked ham, cubed
- 1 medium carrot, diced
- 1 large onion, chopped
- 2-3 garlic cloves, minced
- 2 bay leaves
- 5 cups water
- Salt and pepper to taste

Directions

1. Take your slow cooker and lay ingredients in rows - do not stir. Place peas, then cooked ham, carrots, onions, garlic, bay leaves. Season with salt and pepper and pour in water.
2. Cover and cook on high for 3,5 - 4 hours until peas are cooked and tender.
3. Remove and discard bay leaves, stir to combine and serve.

Vegetable and Lentil Soup

Prep time: 8 minutes, cook time: 6 hours, servings: 6

Ingredients

- 3 large carrots, chopped
- 1 small parsnip, chopped
- 4 celery stalks, chopped
- 2 medium-sized onions, chopped
- 3 garlic cloves, minced
- 1 cup lentils, rinsed and drained
- 6 cups vegetable broth
- 1 tablespoon tamari
- 1 teaspoon salt
- ¼ teaspoon ground black pepper
- Freshly chopped herbs on your preference for garnish
- 1 tablespoon olive oil

Directions

1. Switch your slow cooker to a sauté mode and sprinkle with olive oil.
2. Add onions and garlic and sauté for 5 minutes, stirring occasionally.
3. Add celery, carrots, parsnip, and lentils. Pour in broth and season with salt and pepper.
4. Close the lid and cook on low for 6 hours.
    Garnish with freshly chopped herbs and enjoy.ley and serve.

Spicy Bean Soup with Turkey

Prep time: 7 minutes, cook time: 4 ½ hours, servings: 5-6

Ingredients

- 1 pound turkey breast, cooked and cubed
- 2 cans (15 oz each) beans, rinsed
- 3 cups chicken stock
- 1 can (10 oz) diced tomatoes with green chilies
- 1 cup salsa
- ½ teaspoon dried basil
- ½ teaspoon smoked paprika
- ¼ teaspoon cayenne pepper
- ¼ teaspoon curry
- A pinch of salt

Directions

1. Cut cooked turkey into 1-inch cubes and place to a slow cooker. Add beans and diced tomatoes, stir in salsa and pour in chicken stock.
2. Add herbs and spices and stir to combine.
3. Cover and cook on low for 5 hours.
4. Serve hot.

Kale Soup with Italian Sausage

Prep time: 15 minutes, cook time: 6 hours, servings: 7-8

Ingredients

- 6 cups chopped fresh kale
- 1 pound Italian sausage (you may use any on your preference)
- 3 large carrots, chopped
- 1 large onion, chopped
- 4 garlic cloves, minced
- 2 cans (15 oz) kidney beans, rinsed and drained
- 1 can (28 oz) crushed tomatoes
- 1 teaspoon dried basil
- 1 tablespoon olive oil
- Salt and black pepper to taste
- ¼ cup grated Parmesan for serving

Directions

1. Heat the olive oil in a large skillet over high heat and cook sausage for 5-7 minutes until no longer pink, breaking into small pieces.
2. Place browned sausage in a slow cooker pot. Add kale, carrots, onions and garlic. Stir in beans and tomatoes and mix well.
3. Cover lid and cook on low for 6 hours until sausage and veggies are tender.
4. Serve warm and top with grated Parmesan.

Potato & Beef Soup

Prep time: 25 minutes, cook time: 6 hours, servings: 7-8

Ingredients

- 1 pound ground beef
- 2 large onions, chopped
- 4 large potatoes, peeled and cut into 1-inch cubes
- 3 large carrots, chopped
- 4 garlic cloves, minced
- ½ cup all-purpose flour
- 4 cups chicken or beef stock
- 1 cup skimmed milk
- ½ cup low-fat sour cream
- 12 ounces process cheese, cubed
- 2 tablespoons dried basil
- 1 tablespoon dried thyme
- 2 tablespoons olive oil
- ¼ teaspoon black pepper
- 1 teaspoon salt

Directions

1. Heat the olive oil in a skillet over medium-high heat and cook chopped onion for 3-5 minutes. Add ground beef and cook until no longer pink, for about 5-7 minutes.
2. Whisk flour and 2 cups of stock and pour in beef mixture. Bring to a boil and cook stirring occasionally for 2-3 minutes.
3. Place the mixture to a slow cooker. Add potatoes, carrots, dried herbs, garlic and remaining stock.
4. Cover and cook for 5-6 hours until vegetables are tender.

5. Add cheese and pour in milk. Cook for 30 minutes more until cheese melted.
6. Stir in sour cream before serving.

Chicken Tomato Soup

Prep time: 10 minutes, cook time: 4 ½ hours, servings: 7-8

Ingredients

- 1 pound chicken breasts
- 1 large onion, chopped
- 2 large potatoes, peeled and cubed
- 1 small carrot, chopped
- 2-3 garlic cloves, crushed
- 2 cups frozen corn
- 1 can (10 oz) tomato puree
- 4 cups chicken stock
- 1 can (10 oz) diced tomatoes
- 1 teaspoon ground cumin
- 1 teaspoon chili powder
- 1/8 teaspoon cayenne pepper
- ½ to 1 teaspoon salt
- ½ cup fresh chopped parsley

Directions

1. Cut chicken into 1-inch cubes. Also peel and cut potatoes into 1-inch cubes. Add all ingredients to a slow cooker and season with herbs and spices.
2. Pour in chicken stock, cover and cook on low for 4-5 hours.
3. Sprinkle with freshly chopped parsley and serve hot.

Black Beans & Ham Soup

Prep time: 15 minutes, cook time: 4 hours, servings: 6-8

Ingredients

- 1 pound cooked ham, cubed
- 2 medium-sized onions, chopped
- 2 garlic cloves, minced
- 1 small carrot, chopped
- 1 can (15 oz) diced tomatoes with juices
- 3 cans (15 oz each) black beans, drained
- 4 cups chicken or beef stock
- 3 tablespoons dried herb mix (thyme, basil, cilantro)
- 1 tablespoon olive oil
- Salt and black pepper to taste
- Sour cream for topping

Directions

1. In the large skillet heat the olive oil over high heat. Cook cubed ham for 4-5 minutes until browned. Transfer to a slow cooker.

2. Add onions, carrots, and garlic, stir in tomatoes with juices and beans, pour in stock. Season with herbs, salt, and pepper and stir to combine.
3. Cover and cook on high for 4 hours until beans tender.
4. Top with sour cream if desired, serve and enjoy!

Conclusion

Thank you again for downloading my cookbook! I Hope this book helps you to know more interesting and tasty recipes or inspire you to create your own unique dishes.

www.ingramcontent.com/pod-product-compliance
Lightning Source LLC
Chambersburg PA
CBHW071436070526
44578CB00001B/106